POWER SHOVELS

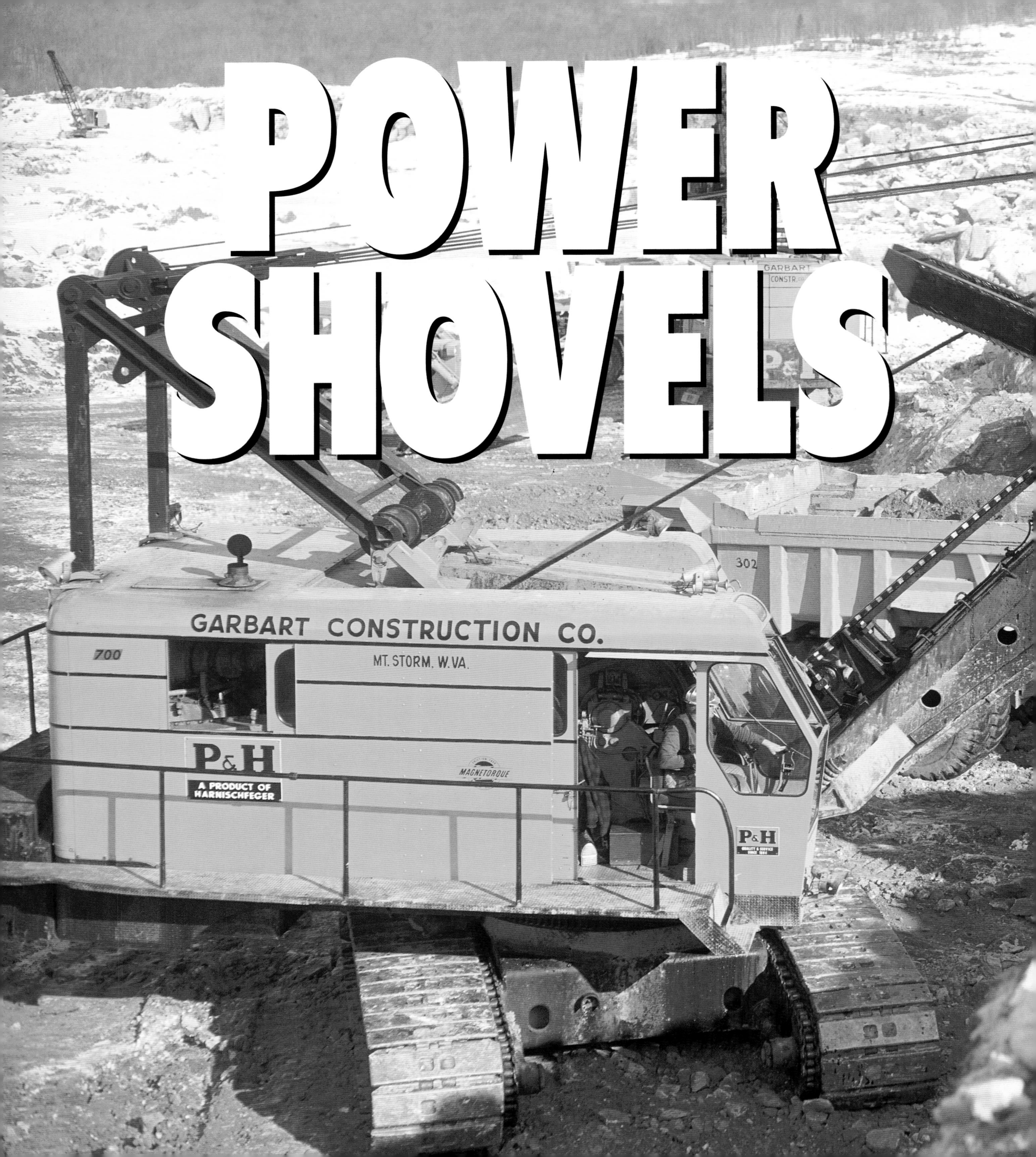
GARBART CONSTR.
302
GARBART CONSTRUCTION CO.
700
MT. STORM. W.VA.
P&H
A PRODUCT OF HARNISCHFEGER
MAGNETORQUE
P&H

ERIC C. ORLEMANN

MOTORBOOKS
INTERNATIONAL

This edition first published in 2003 by Motorbooks International, an imprint of MBI Publishing Company, Galtier Plaza, Suite 200, 380 Jackson Street, St. Paul, MN 55101-3885 USA

Motorbooks International titles are also available at discounts in bulk quantity for industrial or sales-promotional use. For details write to Special Sales Manager at Motorbooks International Wholesalers & Distributors, Galtier Plaza, Suite 200, 380 Jackson Street, St. Paul, MN 55101-3885 USA.

ISBN: 0-7603-1104-8

On the front cover:
Bucyrus Erie 3850-B 140-cubic-yard Dipper
Probably one of the most recognized publicity photographs ever taken in regard to a stripping shovel is this image of the Bucyrus Erie 3850-B Lot II dipper from Peabody Coal's River King No. 6 Mine, in November 1964. As one might imagine, nothing shows off its monstrous 140-cubic-yard capacity better than a man standing next to it for scale. *Bucyrus International*

On the frontispiece:
Bucyrus Erie 50-B
There was a time during the early part of the 20th century that construction and mining steam shovels were as common as steam locomotives. But like the steam engines of old, the steam-powered shovels today are but a fading memory of what once was. Thankfully, a few survive today, such as this impressive 1929-vintage Bucyrus Erie 50-B steam shovel. Owned by Bill Rudicill of Petersburg, Kentucky, it is presently the largest operable steam shovel in North America. *Eric C. Orlemann (ECO)*

On the title page:
P&H 1055
This P&H 1055 diesel-powered shovel is at work in the early 1960s loading haulers in the cold of winter. Today, the scene in the quarry and mining industry is much the same, but the shovels and trucks that work in them have gotten a whole lot larger in their capacities and overall sizes. *Author's collection*

On the back cover:
The only "super-stripping" shovel preserved for public display is the Bucyrus Erie 1850-B originally built for the Pittsburg & Midway Coal Mining Company in 1963. P&M donated the shovel in 1983 to the nonprofit organization of Big Brutus, Inc., which was entrusted with the care and restoration of the giant. In 1985 the shovel was opened to the public. It is shown here in August 1998. *ECO*

Edited by Steve Gansen
Designed by LeAnn Kuhlmann

Printed in Hong Kong

CONTENTS

ACKNOWLEDGMENTS

Doing a project such as *Power Shovels* requires a fair amount of lead-time, as well as the cooperation of a host of individuals who ultimately would like to see you succeed in your mission. The mining industry as a whole has always been supportive of my book endeavors, and I am glad to say, this one is no exception. Without the help of the following individuals and the companies they represent, this book would not have been possible. They are: Kent Henschen of Bucyrus International; Mark Dietz, Art Beyersdorf, Jordan Johnston, and Al Strom of P&H Mining; Merilee S. Hunt and K. Peter Winkel of Liebherr Mining Equipment; J. Peter Ahrenkiel and Jess Ewing of Terex Mining; Lee Haak of Komatsu America; Bryce Short of Transwest Mining Systems; Christine L. Taylor, Vic Svec, Cindy S. Miller, Beth C. Sutton, and William A. Vance of Peabody Energy; Greg Dundas and Bob Heimann of Powder River Coal Company; Charlene Murdock, Michael J. Stevermer, and Rafael A. Nunez of Kennecott Energy; Thomas J. Lien, Kurt Cost, Kevin Avery, Larry Vail, Bob Davis, and William M. Dalton of RAG Coal West; Ray Reipas and Paul Sirois of Suncor Energy; Bonnie Clemetson of Thunder Basin Coal Company; and Greg Halinda.

I also thank the many photographers and researchers from around the world that have so graciously supplied additional images to this project. All I can say is that their work speaks for itself. Thanks to Dale Davis, Peter N. Grimshaw, Michael Hubert, Mike Haskins, Jon Kuss, Gary Middlebrook, Urs Peyer, Les P. Kent, Stewart Halperin, Randall Hyman, and Allen Campbell.

I also express my sincerest gratitude toward: Bill Rudicill and Harvey F. Pelley for all of the time and effort they put toward getting the 50-B steam shovel up and running in time for such a tight shooting schedule. A big thanks is also in order to Jeff Solley for additional research information and Thomas Berry of the Historical Construction Equipment Association (HCEA) for supplying needed historical material.

Last but not least, I thank Keith Haddock of Park Communications. Keith and I have worked together over the years on a host of related projects. There is no one else in the world I trust more when it comes to advice and research help in the mining industry than Keith. Whether it is a rare photo or some odd little fact about some long-forgotten piece of equipment, chances are good that Keith has the correct answer at hand. Thanks again.

—*Eric C. Orlemann*
Decatur, Illinois 2003

Bucyrus Erie 3850-B Lot II
Peabody's Bucyrus Erie 3850-B
Lot II shovel takes a massive
210-ton bite of overburden with
its 140-cubic-yard-capacity dipper
at the River King No. 6 Mine in
the spring of 1992. It would be
parked in September of that
same year. *Stewart Halperin*

INTRODUCTION

What makes us who we are, our likes and dislikes, can often be tracked back to a single occurrence or a series of specific events in our lives. Some are quite abstract; others are more straightforward. Like so many other children of my time from the early 1960s, I spent the first few years of my life as the foreman of a busy earthmoving job site known as a sandbox. Here, holes were dug and then filled in, over and over. Lincoln Log buildings would go up and then come crashing down. Bridges built over raging rivers were no problem with the aid of an erector set and a garden hose. Everything was possible. There was nothing my earthmoving equipment fleet could not do when fueled with my unlimited youthful imagination.

The lessons in the sandbox gave me hands-on experience in the process of moving material in the most simple of terms. The next event that shaped my view was a bit more cerebral. Around the age of four, I was introduced to the world of *Mike Mulligan and His Steam Shovel*. This story of an Irish operator and his beloved steam shovel, Mary Anne, written in 1939 by Virginia Lee Burton, is considered a true classic in children's literature. It was while watching the *Captain Kangaroo Show* one morning on TV that the good captain (Bob Keeshan) read the story of the shovel operator and his machine to his viewers while still images of the book's artwork were displayed on the screen. I was hooked. From then on, anything that resembled Mike Mulligan's shovel in the real world was referred to as a "steam" shovel. If it had a bucket, made smoke, and could dig, it had to be a steam shovel. It was some years before I realized that there were no more steam-powered shovels, only diesel and electric. Why no one corrected me any sooner is beyond me. I suppose a four-year-old calling anything with a bucket a steam shovel was considered cute. After all, no one was dispelling the notion that Santa Claus was not real either.

It is now almost 40 years since these humble beginnings first took hold in my subconscious. Throughout my professional career in industrial marketing and advertising, it has always been the large mining equipment industry that has never failed to pique my curiosity. The distant memories of Mike Mulligan have been replaced with the reality of stripping shovels 21 stories tall, whose bucket capacities are measured in the hundreds of tons, loading shovels so large that they can fill a 360-ton hauler with just three swings of its bucket. Steam shovels have given way to giant diesel and electric machines, yet both past and present, power shovels have been the front line in the creation of our modern society.

What exactly is a power shovel? Simply stated, it is any type of front-digging and -loading device incorporating a boom and a dipper that is powered by some onboard means. This can include steam, gasoline, diesel, and electric power. The machine can have a chain, steel rope, or cable hoist design or be powered by hydraulics. Power shovels fall under the broad category of excavators. Excavators include all types of earthmoving digging and conveying machines, including backhoes, bucket wheels, and draglines. But it is the power shovels that are the most easily recognized, especially the cable machines. When one sees a shovel in operation, there is no doubt as to what its primary purpose in life is. Its basic design has not changed all that much from its origins dating back to 1835. It is not as easy to witness a power shovel in action today as it once was. As the shovels have increased in size, they have been largely confined to quarry and mining operations, out of sight from most people. In jobs where a cable shovel or backhoe was once common, the hydraulic excavator and wheel loader now reign supreme. Only at the top of the excavator food chain does the cable shovel still hold sway.

This book explores the world of the large cable and hydraulic shovels that inhabit the world's quarry and mining industries, both past and present. These include loading shovels, both cable and hydraulic, as well as the massive stripping shovels. In addition to the large hydraulic shovels mentioned, their backhoe-configured counterparts are also covered to give a more precise description of the machine model itself. The main emphasis of this book is the large quarry- and mining-type shovels, including their early beginnings in the steam era, and not the smaller, contractor-sized machines. Because of the sheer numbers of models built over the decades, it was necessary to limit the scope of this project to the largest and most historically significant shovel types, as well as manufacturers, for their respective time periods. The smaller shovels are no less important than their larger brothers, but it is without question the giants of the earthmoving industry that capture our imagination and fill us with amazement and awe.

At work in 1997 is Peabody Energy's Marion 5900 stripping shovel at its Lynnville mining operations in Indiana. With its massive 112-cubic-yard dipper (105 cubic yards originally), the giant stripper has just taken a 168-ton bite of overburden, as it uncovers a large seam of coal. *Allen Campbell*

Chapter One

THE STEAM ERA

During the early 1800s, both in the United States and in Europe, the process of digging and moving earth for construction and building endeavors was still based largely on man and animal power. It was relatively cheap and in large supply. A man with a shovel, a pick, and a wheelbarrow was as good as it got in most instances. In England, men of this profession were often referred to as "navigators," or "navvies" for short. These pick-and-shovel laborers were first associated with the building and excavating of waterway canals, but this soon gave way to the construction of railroads. As time went by, these hard-working and hard-living men would simply be known as "railway navvies."

During the 1830s William Smith Otis felt that there had to be a better, more efficient and less labor-intensive means to the process of digging and loading large quantities of earth. Born on September 20, 1813, in Pelham, Massachusetts, Otis was of English decent, and his family tree in America dated back to 1631. Otis probably developed his interest in construction because his father had been a contractor for many years in Pennsylvania. At about age 20, while living in Philadelphia, Otis joined the contracting firm of Carmichael and Fairbanks, in which he became a partner in 1834. That year Carmichael, Fairbanks, and Otis successfully bid on a contract for the construction of a section of the Boston and Providence Railroad. To carry out his duties involving this contract, Otis made a temporary residence move to Canton, Massachusetts.

While working on the Boston and Providence contract in 1835, Otis started to tinker around with the idea of building some sort of land-based excavating machine. Up until this time, all mechanized excavating designs were of a dredge-type nature. Otis, with the assistance of his friend Charles Howe French, was able to fabricate the world's first steam shovel excavator. The device's design was rather simple: it had a cable-supported mast from which the main boom was suspended. A dipper handle with bucket was attached to the boom and was raised and lowered by means of a steam-powered double-drum chain hoist. The entire structure was supported by four wheels on steel rail lines. To rotate the boom for dumping, ropes were attached on the right and left. Two men, one on either side of the boom, then pulled on the lines to swing the bucket into its dumping area and then back into digging position. These men were also responsible for tripping the bucket door latch.

Once Otis and French completed the prototype steam shovel, also referred to as a power

Bucyrus Erie 50-B
This Bucyrus Erie 50-B steam shovel was originally built in 1929 and sold to the Kentucky-Virginia Stone Company of Middlesboro, Kentucky, for the tidy sum of $22,500. The shovel worked at the company's limestone quarry in Wheeler, Virginia, from May 1929 to early 1951. *ECO*

Otis Steam Shovel

In 1835, William Smith Otis built the world's first land-based "steam shovel"-type excavator. This illustration from 1841 by S. Rufus Mason, a Philadelphia-based drafting instructor, was of the second machine built by Otis, often referred to as an Otis "Philadelphia" Shovel.

Author's collection

shovel, French demonstrated it in Worcester, Massachusetts, while working on a section of the Norwich and Worcester Railroad. During the trials of the first machine, a few shortcomings in the design made themselves known, but none caused the power shovel concept to be abandoned. Though a steam shovel was a rather revolutionary technical achievement in 1835, one has to remember the time period in American history in which it was conceived. Railroads were still confined to the far eastern part of the country. The California gold rush was 14 years away, the Civil War would begin in 26 years, and the invention of the first incandescent light bulb was still 44 years

in the future. The steam shovel was a machine that would ultimately lead the country into a time of great industrialization in the late 1870s.

Upon completion of his duties in Canton in late 1835, Otis moved back to Philadelphia. There he started work on an improved shovel design. Otis enlisted the aid of his cousin, S. Rufus Mason, who was an instructor in drafting, to help produce a complete set of drawings of his new design. Finding it beyond their means to build the machine themselves, Otis contracted with the firm of Garret and Eastwick (soon to be renamed Eastwick and Harrison) to fabricate the improved power shovel for him. By 1837, Eastwick and Harrison had completed the design for the "Philadelphia" shovel. On June 15, 1836, Otis first applied for patent rights on his "Crane Excavator for Excavating and Removing Earth," but a fire at the U.S. Patent Office destroyed the first set of application documents. A new set was filed on October 27, 1838. Otis was officially granted Patent No. 1089 on his shovel on February 24, 1839.

Not long after its completion in 1837, Otis put the first "Philadelphia" shovel to work on a project for the Western Railroad of Massachusetts. But Otis would not live to see his power shovel concept reach full maturity. While working on the railroad project, Otis contracted typhus fever. He died on November 13, 1839, in Westfield, Massachusetts, almost nine months after receiving the patent on his invention. Otis was only 26 years old when he died, leaving a promising historic legacy unfulfilled; but his initial contribution to the technological advancement of the earthmoving industry is without question. It would be up to others to carry on, including his wife, Elizabeth, who was now in full control of her late husband's shovel patent.

After Otis died, Eastwick and Harrison went on to build seven "Philadelphia" shovels by 1843. Of the seven, one was shipped to England and four to Russia, leaving only two in the United States. That's how it remained for the next few years. The development of the steam shovel came to a standstill. Because of the large numbers of skilled immigrant laborers, there was simply not a cry from the railroad and building industries for a mechanized shovel to move earth. Another stumbling block was that the patent on the Otis shovel was held by his widow, which stifled other possible manufacturers from building a steam shovel design of their own. But soon, many realized that a mechanized land excavator was the way of the future for meeting the growing demands of an ever expanding nation.

On March 23, 1844, Elizabeth Everett Otis married Oliver S. Chapman. He had been a close friend of the Otis family and had originally met Elizabeth's husband, William, in Canton while working as a contractor on the Boston and Providence Railroad project in 1834. Though Chapman had been retired as a contractor for a few years, just after marrying in 1844 he found

himself drawn back into the earthmoving business. His business grew to such an extent that by the mid-1850s, Chapman needed power shovels of his own. Chapman was a wise businessman. Even before he had a need for steam shovels of his own, he had persuaded Elizabeth to file a patent extension on her late husband's shovel in 1853, further protecting the original design for years to come. Not a manufacturer in his own right, Chapman enlisted the aid of the Globe Iron Works of South Boston to begin production of the Otis shovel once again. These machines were referred to as Otis "Boston" shovels. In addition to this, Chapman himself was granted a patent in 1867, No. 63857, on "certain improvements to the Otis shovel," as the document read. One of the key improvements was the utilization of a chain crowd mechanism to supply force to the bucket digging edge. As railroad construction expanded at a record pace, so did the sales of Otis (also identified as Otis-Chapman) steam shovels. But it would not be long before other companies figured out how

Barnhart's Steam Shovel-Style A
The Barnhart's Steam Shovel-Style A was one of Marion's more popular railroad-type shovel designs dating back to 1883. The 1.25-cubic-yard shovel shown was originally sold to the E. H. France Company in Bloomville, Ohio, in 1886. In all, approximately 416 units of the Style A had been built when production ended in 1906. *HCEA*

Above: **Bucyrus Erie 50-B**
Originally introduced in 1922, the Bucyrus Erie 50-B was one of the premier excavators in the 2-cubic-yard class for its time. The 50-B could be configured as a shovel, a dragline, a clamshell, or a crane. Approximate working weight was 71 tons in shovel form. *ECO*

Right: **Marion Model 40**
The shovel crew of a Marion Model 40 working in Virginia in the early 1910s takes a quick break to pose for the camera with a fully loaded dipper. The 1.25-cubic-yard Model 40 was built from 1908 to 1912. *HCEA*

Left: **Bucyrus Erie 50-B**
The Bucyrus Erie 50-B was available not only as a steam-powered excavator, it could also be ordered with diesel or electric power sources. When configured with steam, its boiler could either be coal fired, as the one shown, or oil fired. *ECO*

Below: **Bucyrus No. 0**
Largest of Bucyrus' early railroad-type shovel designs was its No. 0. Introduced in 1888, the 2.25-cubic-yard shovel was soon eclipsed by far larger Bucyrus models, such as its 5-cubic-yard "95-TON" from 1899. This image of a Bucyrus No. 0 is from 1890. *Keith Haddock collection*

to build power shovels of their own to capitalize on such a profitable and wanted machine for railroad construction contracts.

By 1878, industrialization in the United States was in full swing. Construction, railroad expansion, mining, and steel production were all on the rise. Larger and more efficient railroad-type steam shovels were also in high demand. As the years progressed, the steam shovel was viewed less as a primary railroad building tool and waterway dredge, and more of a quarry and mining machine. As an example, from 1880 to 1900, steel production in the United States increased dramatically from a yearly output of 1,400,000 tons to more than 11,000,000 tons. The mining of large quantities of iron ore was essential to this increase in steel production, made possible only by means of the power shovel. The first steam shovel of record to mine iron ore was in 1891. Other mining firsts for the shovel included stripping coal in 1877 and digging copper ore in 1896. By 1905, the power shovel was a common sight in numerous quarry operations across North America.

Bucyrus 78C

In 1922, Bucyrus started to offer crawler mounts for use on its railroad-type shovel designs, freeing them from the constraints of the steel rail. This 3.5-cubic-yard Bucyrus 78C, introduced in 1915, has been retrofitted with two outrigger-type crawlers in the front and two crawlers mounted in the rear under the main frame. *Keith Haddock collection*

During this time of industrialization in the United States, steam shovel manufacturers started to spring up in the Midwest, especially in Ohio. Across the Atlantic, builders of railroad-type excavating shovels also came into being in England. One of the most popular of these English firms was the Ruston, Proctor and Company, established in 1858. The firm built its first steam shovel, referred to as the "Dunbar and Ruston Steam Navvy," in 1874, which actually shipped to a paying customer in 1875. In 1876, the company was also granted a patent on a full-revolving shovel design. The concept was way ahead of its time, but in the end, the company never proceeded to a prototype version in-the-iron. Eventually, in 1918, the company became Ruston and Hornsby.

In America, there were quite a few companies that built railroad-type steam shovels. Some of the more notable manufacturers included Osgood Dredge Company (1875) of Troy, New York; and Ohio Steam Shovel Company (1903) of Toledo (later, Ohio Power Shovel of Lima, Ohio, builders of the Lima line of excavators). Another company of special note was Toledo Foundry and Machine,

also from Toledo, Ohio, which in 1877 was the first to mount a shovel on a standard-gauge railroad flatcar. This would help standardize the building of railroad-type shovels and their ability to be used across a wide variety of the nation's rail lines. In 1882, this company became Vulcan Iron Works. But of all the early American companies, two stand out from the rest: Bucyrus Foundry and Manufacturing, and Marion Steam Shovel. These two firms, more than any other, laid the groundwork for power shovels of incredible productivity, as well as size, for more than 100 years to come. And a rivalry would commence between the two manufacturers that became legendary in the earthmoving industry.

Bucyrus Foundry and Manufacturing was founded in 1880 by Dan P. Eells and a group of business associates. In 1889, the company changed its name to the Bucyrus Steam Shovel and Dredge Company. Originally located in Bucyrus, Ohio, the company was later moved to South Milwaukee, Wisconsin, where manufacturing commenced in 1893. In 1897, the company changed its name to The Bucyrus Company.

Bucyrus Erie 50-B

After the 50-B was parked in the spring of 1951, it remained idle at the Kentucky-Virginia Stone Company's shop until it was purchased by its present owner, Belleview Sand and Gravel, in June 1994. It was then moved to Belleview's operations in Petersburg, Kentucky. *ECO*

Above: **Marion Model 28**
Along with railroad-type mountings, Marion also offered steel traction wheels as an option for most of its early shovel offerings, such as this full-revolving 5/8-cubic-yard Model 28. Built from 1911 to 1919, it proved to be a popular model for the company, with 402 eventually being produced. *HCEA*

Right: **Marion Model 28**
Starting around 1916, Marion Steam Shovel offered crawler track assemblies for use on its smaller line of excavators. The first was its Model 28, though its larger, heavy-duty, railroad-type shovels would not get crawler mountings until 1923.
Author's collection

Bucyrus built its first steam shovel in 1882. Referred to as the No. 1 "Thompson Iron Steam Shovel and Derrick," the design was a railroad-type shovel for the Ohio Central Railroad. So successful was the "Thompson" that 59 were eventually built by 1889. Bucyrus was now solidly in the steam shovel business.

Bucyrus' archrival, Marion, got its start in 1883, with steam shovel operator Henry M. Barnhart of Marion, Ohio. Dissatisfied with many of the available shovels of the day, Barnhart decided to build a better one. Enlisting the aid of Edward Huber of the Huber Manufacturing Company, located in Marion, Barnhart was able to

Above: **Bucyrus Erie 50-B**
In 1951 the previous owners of this 50-B had completely renovated the boiler and were getting it ready to go back to work, when they decided to replace the steam-powered shovel with a new diesel model. Though the shovel had sat idle for some 43 years, it was in remarkably good condition, with all of its original parts still in place. *ECO*

Above right: **Bucyrus Erie 50-B**
Steam shovels like this Bucyrus Erie 50-B seemed almost alive when in operation. The hissing of the steam, the belching of the smokestack, and the clanking of the bucket and tracks, all would give one's senses a thorough workout. This detailed image of the back of the boom shows the smaller steam-thrusting engine that supplied the necessary crowd force for digging through these large gear sets located on either side of the boom. *ECO*

build his dream steam shovel. Called the "Barnhart's Steam Shovel and Wrecking Car," the railroad-type machine was an immediate success and was sold to the Jackson and Mackinaw Railroad. In 1884, Barnhart, Huber, and business associate George W. King founded the Marion Steam Shovel Company, also based in Marion. Steam shovel manufacturers would come and go, but Marion, along with Bucyrus, proved to be the best of the breed.

Marion Steam Shovel went on to introduce quite a few railroad-type shovel models, ranging from approximately 25- to 137-ton operating weights, with bucket capacities of .75 to 6.0 cubic yards. Early models carried a letter designation, such as the 1.25-cubic-yard Barnhart's Steam Shovel-Style A of 1886. Starting in 1900, a numerical model designation was introduced, which was based on the approximate shipping weight of the shovel. Also, the machines themselves were now referred to as "Marion Shovel" and not "Barnhart Steam Shovel." The first to carry the new designation in 1900 was the 3.5-cubic-yard Model 80. Some of the company's more popular railroad shovels included the 2.5-cubic-yard Model G from 1897 (124 built), the 1.25-yard Model 20 from 1901 (228 built), the 5.0-yard Model 91 from 1902 (131 built), the 1.5-yard Model 41 from 1912 (75 built), and the 3.25-yard Model 70 from 1912 (74 built). The largest of all Marion railroad-type shovels was its 6.0-yard, 137-ton Model 100. It was in production from

1909 to 1926, with 39 listed as being built. The company shipped its last railroad shovel in 1931, a Model 61. Originally introduced in 1912, the Model 61 was a 2.5-cubic-yard machine. In all, 131 Model 61 shovels were sold.

The basic Marion railroad-type shovel was equipped with a boom capable of an approximate 200-degree swing radius. But in 1908, the company introduced the smaller Model 30 and 35 shovels, which featured full 360-degree revolving upper works. Though most were coal fired, Marion offered many of its more popular models with electric power, such as its Model 51 and 91 shovels. Some of the smaller units could also be specified with steel traction wheels. These were usually required for use where the working ground conditions were of an extremely hard nature, making it impractical to lay steel track. These conditions were often encountered in iron ore, coal, and silica rock operations. Starting in 1923, Marion offered crawler truck assemblies on its railroad shovel offerings as retrofit kits for owners wishing to convert their older railroad shovels into more practical crawler-type excavators.

Though Marion designed quite a number of railroad-type shovels while that breed of equipment was in production, Bucyrus produced even more model types during the same time. No less than 37 separate model types of the larger railroad shovels were offered between 1882 and 1929. And this number does not even include the smaller

full-revolving rail-mounted machines. It is no wonder that during the digging of the Panama Canal, Bucyrus supplied the bulk of the railroad-type steam shovels in use. During that project's run from 1904 to 1914, some 255 million cubic yards of material were moved by means of 77 Bucyrus shovels, 24 Marion shovels, and 1 Thew steam shovel. It was an enormous engineering feat for its day.

Bucyrus went through three distinct periods of identifying its railroad-type shovels. In the beginning, they were referred to with single digit numbers, such as the first "Thompson" shovel, which carried the No. 1 designation. Other models included the No. 2 in 1886, the No. 3 in 1888, and the No. 4 in 1892. Largest of the early machines was the 2.25-cubic-yard No. 0 from 1888. Starting around 1897, new model introductions now had the word "*TON*" in them, the first of which was the 60-TON. The largest in this series was the 95-TON

from 1899, which was a 5-cubic-yard shovel. This changed again around 1906, when new models either had a "*C*" (chain-hoist) or "*R*" (rope-hoist) in their titles. The first of these shovels was the 2-cubic-yard 45C. The largest rope-hoist machine listed as being built was the 3-yard 70R in 1909. But the largest of all Bucyrus railroad shovels was its 6-yard 110C from the early 1920s. Weighing 131 tons, it was in direct competition with the 137-ton Marion Model 100. Bucyrus eventually ended production of its railroad shovels in 1929. The last shovel of this kind sold by the company was its popular 3-yard 68C. Originally introduced in 1915, the last 68C was shipped from inventory to a customer in 1930.

Though Marion had introduced its first small, full-revolving shovels to the marketplace ahead of Bucyrus, they would soon catch up in the early 1910s with models of their own. Bucyrus introduced its first two full-revolving shovels in 1912,

Bucyrus 80-B
Introduced in 1921, the Bucyrus 80-B was the largest shovel model the company had ever offered with crawler mountings as standard equipment up until that time. Weighing 100 tons with a 2.5-cubic-yard dipper, the 80-B made an excellent shovel for general excavation work and was a good coal-stripping machine. The 80-B was available with steam or electric power and could be ordered as a dragline. Production came to an end on the model line in 1929. *Author's collection*

the 5/8-cubic-yard 14-B and the 7/8-cubic-yard 18-B. They added slightly larger shovels of this type in 1914: the 1.25-cubic-yard 25-B and the 1.5-cubic-yard 35-B. All of these steam shovel types had full 360-degree swing capabilities and were configured as rail-mounted machines in standard form, with the option of steel traction wheels. Not long after the introductions of the 25-B and 35-B, crawler track assemblies started to be offered instead of the rail mountings. Other popular full-revolving steam shovel models included the .75-cubic-yard 20-B in 1922, the 1.0-yard 30-B in 1920, and the 1.0-yard 31-B and 1.25-yard 41-B, both in 1926. Others were the 1.5-yard 42-B in 1930, the popular 2.0-yard 50-B in 1922, the 2.5-yard 80-B in 1921, and the 3.0-yard 100-B in 1926. In addition to steam, many of these shovels could also be configured for gasoline, diesel, and electric operation. In the case of the 50-B, which was in production until 1937, it was offered in a steam version, either coal or oil fired, as an electric-powered shovel or as a diesel-engined machine. Each offered to meet a customer's specific working requirements.

Marion was able to counter most of the full-revolving steam shovels offered by Bucyrus in the 1910s and early 1920s. The only exceptions to this were the largest of the Bucyrus models, the 80-B and 100-B. After Marion launched its Model 30 and 35 full-revolving shovels in 1908,

Above: **Bucyrus Erie 50-B**
The operator's cab on shovels of this type were open to the elements, which allowed all of the day's dust and dirt in, as well as any foul weather. The operators and firemen of these machines certainly had their hands full with a shovel the size of the 50-B. At the controls of this Bucyrus Erie 50-B is Bill Rudicill, owner of Belleview Sand and Gravel. Born in 1939, Bill has been in the earthmoving trade since he was 16. In 1983 he established Belleview Sand and Gravel, on the Ohio River. *ECO*

Left: **Bucyrus Erie 50-B**
The steam version of the 50-B was equipped with a locomotive-type boiler with a large heating surface that made better use of the coal during burning. Working pressure was set at 125 pounds per square inch. A fireman in back of the shovel housing was responsible for keeping the firebox fueled, as well as keeping an eye on the water level and steam pressure. *ECO*

the company continued to introduce new models with increased capacities. In 1911, the 5/8-yard Model 28 was introduced. In 1912, it launched the 1.0-yard Model 31 and 1.5-yard Model 36. Initially, these models were built as rail-mounted shovels, with the option of steel traction wheels. Starting in 1916, Marion started to offer tracked crawler assemblies for its smaller excavators, first on the Model 28 and then on designs already in production. Other models of Marion full-revolving shovels included the 1.5-yard Model 32 and 1.75-yard Model 37, both in 1922; the 1.0-yard Type 7 in 1926; the 1.0-yard Type 440 in 1927; and the 1.25-yard Type 450 and 2.0-yard Type 480, both in 1928. The Type 480 was Marion's largest conventional tracked steam shovel design. The best selling of all

the early Marion shovels of this type was its .75-yard Model 21 from 1919. Produced until 1926, approximately 810 units of the little scrappy shovel were sold.

Most of Marion's smaller shovel offerings during this time period could be configured to run on steam, gasoline, gasoline-electric, diesel, diesel-electric, and electric power. Adding to their versatility, many could be configured not only with shovel fronts, but dragline, clamshell, and crane attachments. This could also be said of the Bucyrus machines offered during this time period.

Though competition did exist from other manufacturers of steam excavators at the time, Marion and Bucyrus were the dominant players.

Bucyrus Erie 50-B
The 50-B shovel's standard dipper capacity was 2 cubic yards. The bucket was supported by a box-girder, boom-straddling dipper handle, which greatly resisted the twisting strains put upon it while the shovel was digging and swinging. *ECO*

Bucyrus 100-B

The Bucyrus 100-B, introduced in 1926, was, after the 120-B, the second-largest conventional shovel the company offered at the time. With a 3-cubic-yard dipper capacity and a 130-ton working weight, it was the perfect general utility shovel. The 100-B could be ordered as a steam or electric machine and was designed from day one as a crawler excavator. Production on the 100-B ended in 1950.
Author's collection

Bucyrus in particular made some key strategic business moves during this time by acquiring competing firms, which would place the company at the forefront of excavator production in North America. One of Bucyrus' rivals in the manufacture of railroad shovels was Vulcan Steam Shovel Company. Originally referred to as the Vulcan Iron Works dating back to 1882, Vulcan Steam Shovel produced a similar line of excavator offerings to that of Bucyrus, sold under the "Giant" brand name. In 1910, Vulcan and The Bucyrus Company formed a new company entity by the name of the Bucyrus-Vulcan Company. But business being what it is, problems quickly arose concerning management. Finally in 1911, The Bucyrus Company, Bucyrus-Vulcan, and the Atlantic Equipment Company, builders of the Atlantic line

of railroad steam shovels, all combined to form the public firm of Bucyrus Company.

The next major event in Bucyrus' history came on December 31, 1927, when the Erie Steam Shovel Company officially merged into the Bucyrus Company, forming the Bucyrus Erie Company. Erie Steam Shovel, which got its start in Erie, Pennsylvania, in 1883 as the Ball Engine Company, was a well-respected manufacturer of small steam shovel excavators for contractor use. The company introduced its first shovel in 1914, the .75-cubic-yard Erie-B. This was followed in 1916 by the .5-yard Erie-A. Both of these shovel designs were full-revolving, mounted either on rails or with steel traction wheels. In 1921, the company introduced crawler-mounted undercarriages for the first time. The following year, the name of the

firm changed from Ball Engine to Erie Steam Shovel Company. Then in 1925, it released its slightly larger 1.0-yard B-2 "Dreadnaught" shovel series. This was the last model introduced by the company before the formation of Bucyrus Erie. This merger gave Bucyrus the extra manufacturing facilities to make it possible to produce a much wider range of smaller excavator types. The merger is considered not only key in the history of excavators, but also one of the more important events in earthmoving history as a whole.

The shovels that have been discussed so far are primarily smaller to midsized contractor-sized machines, with the larger railroad type utilized for heavy excavating and quarry and mining work. But when these machines were in their prime, there were also shovels of immense proportions that were largely confined to the coal-mining industry. Giants in their day, they eventually gave birth to the largest power shovels the world has ever seen. Behold the stripping shovel.

Bucyrus Erie 50-B
This Bucyrus Erie 50-B is currently the largest operable coal-fired steam shovel in North America. An oil-fired 50-B on historic display in California is not in running condition. Approximately 534 units of the 50-B had been manufactured by the time production ceased in 1937. *ECO*

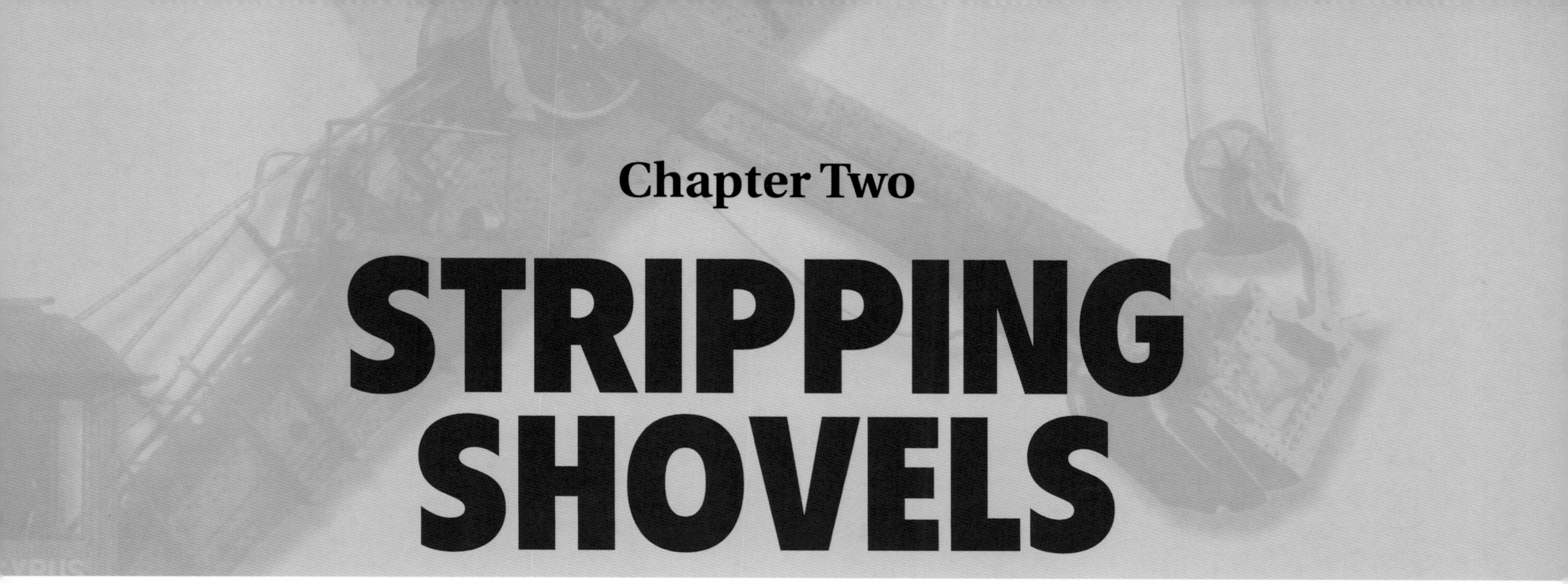

Chapter Two

STRIPPING SHOVELS

As America's industries grew during the early 1900s, larger volumes of raw materials were needed. One of these was coal. Coal was the energy supply that would power most of the industrial expansion of the United States. To get to larger coal seams buried underground, bigger pieces of earthmoving equipment would have to be invented to get the job done. The goal was simple: design and build a shovel big enough to remove the earth, or overburden, covering a coal seam, without the aid of a second shovel. It sounded simple enough, but it would take quite a few innovations from numerous companies to make it a reality.

It was during this time period that the early rail-mounted steam shovel development branched off into two related, but distinct, shovel categories. One was the loading shovel, the other was the stripping shovel. Both machine types evolved simultaneously as the years went by, first with fully revolving frames, and then with crawler mountings to eliminate the steel rail lines. The loading shovel could be configured with a standard-sized or a long-range-type boom. In some instances, the long-range-boomed shovels could be used for stripping purposes, but this did not make them true "stripping" shovels per se. A true stripping shovel was designed from day one as a stripping machine and was not just a retrofitted loading shovel. Power for the loading shovel would go through a series of steps, including steam, electric, gasoline, diesel, and back to electric again. The stripping shovel, on the other hand, would go from steam to electricity only. Because of their sizes, fossil-fueled engines were simply out of the question. Designs for large diesel engines were still years away, and even then, they would still be too small. Only electricity was capable of powering the large stripping shovels after the days of steam were over.

The beginnings of the stripping shovel, as with all power shovels, started with the railroad-type design. In 1899, the Vulcan Steam Shovel Company constructed two railroad-type shovels equipped with longer boom assemblies. Known as "Vulcan Phosphate Specials," they were the earliest shovel design to be considered a long-range stripper; but they still were based on the company's previous railroad 200-degree revolving shovel designs.

In 1900, the English firm John H. Wilson and Company was credited with building the first fully revolving stripping steam shovel. Mounted on rails, it carried a 1.5-cubic-yard dipper on a 70-foot boom and weighed 78 tons. Designed to uncover iron ore, it would have a long and productive life, lasting 54 years. Though extremely crude by today's standards, it was the starting point for giants yet to be.

Bucyrus Erie 3850-B Lot II
The second 3850-B stripping shovel built by Bucyrus Erie, referred to as the Lot II machine, was the largest shovel ever fabricated by the company. Built for Peabody Coal for use at its River King No. 6 Mine, located near Freeburg, Illinois, it was equipped with a massive 140-cubic-yard dipper mounted on a 200-foot boom. It was officially dedicated into service on August 13, 1964, and is shown here at work in May 1967. *Bucyrus International*

A major step in the evolution of the stripping shovel came in 1910, when The Bucyrus Company purchased Vulcan, forming the Bucyrus-Vulcan Company. This transaction would allow Bucyrus to build a stripping shovel of their own. Based on Vulcan designs, the Class 5, as it was known, was the first full-revolving stripping shovel in the United States. The Class 5 was equipped with a 1.5-cubic-yard bucket, mounted to a 55-foot-long boom. Designed for removing overburden, it would find a home working in the coal mines of the Pittsburg, Kansas, area. Eventually, another two of the shovel type would join it, all in this key coal-mining region of the United States.

Though Bucyrus had fielded the first American stripping shovel, it was the Marion Steam Shovel Company that introduced the first stripping shovel design built in America that was truly successful in terms of sales. Known as the Marion Model 250, it was the company's first long-range design built exclusively from day one as a stripping shovel. Assembled in 1911, the steam-powered Model 250 carried a 3.5-cubic-yard dipper and was equipped with a 65-foot boom, far larger than the Bucyrus-

Vulcan Class 5 design from a year earlier. Weighing as much as 150 tons, it was a giant for its day. The first unit was purchased by the Mission Mining Company of Danville, Illinois. Between 1911 and 1913, a total of 19 Marion Model 250 shovels were delivered into service.

The initial success of the Model 250 led Marion to introduce even larger stripping shovel designs. In 1912, even as Model 250s were coming out of the plant, the company introduced its 5-cubic-yard, 260-ton Model 270. In 1913, this was followed up by the 293-ton Model 271. Equipped with the same-sized dipper, it was actually just a beefed-up version of the Model 270. Both designs were steam powered and rail mounted, with full-revolving undercarriages. In 1915, Marion delivered a Model 271 to the Piney Fork Coal Company in Ohio. But what made this shovel so unusual was its use of electric power instead of steam, a first for a stripping shovel, and another engineering first for Marion.

As these designs started to find their way into the marketplace, potential buyers of Bucyrus shovels were finding the much larger Marion

Marion Model 300

Introduced in 1915, the Marion Model 300 was without a doubt the most popular of the company's early rail-mounted stripping shovels. Produced until 1923, there were 74 units built, which included both steam- and electric-powered types. Average dipper capacity was 6 cubic yards, with a working weight of 350 tons. *Author's collection*

Above: Bucyrus 320-B
Largest of the Bucyrus steam-powered stripping shovels was its 320-B from 1923. The 320-B was rated as an 8-cubic-yard stripper and carried a working weight of some 438 tons. Though the 320-B originally was released as a rail-mounted design, crawler assemblies were made available to it in 1925. Production ended on the 320-B series in 1930 with 29 shovels and 8 draglines built. *Keith Haddock collection*

Left: Marion Type 5480
The Marion Type 5480 was the company's first stripping shovel to be offered exclusively with electric power and eight crawler assemblies. Average dipper capacity range was from 12 to 16 cubic yards, with a working weight of 975 tons. Produced from 1928 to 1932, there were 11 shovels and 4 draglines manufactured. *Author's collection*

Bucyrus Erie 1050-B
The Bucyrus Erie 1050-B was the most successful of the company's counterbalanced hoist designed stripping shovels. Originally introduced in 1941, 12 would eventually be placed into service by 1960. This 1050-B shown working in September 1959 at Peabody Coal's Vogue Mine, located near Madisonville, Kentucky, originally shipped from the factory in July 1957 and was the 10th unit built. It was equipped with a 32-cubic-yard dipper. *Author's collection*

stripping machines more to their liking. As one can imagine, this was a situation that Bucyrus was not going to stand for. With a sense of urgency, Bucyrus engineers started to burn the midnight oil as they worked on their drawing boards, designing a shovel to stop Marion's sales advance into the marketplace. Their answer to the Marion machines were the 2.5-cubic-yard, 158-ton 150-B and 3.5-cubic-yard, 220-ton 175-B. Built in 1912, these steam-powered, rail-mounted stripping shovels met the needs of many of its customers for a shovel large enough to remove overburden in coal-mining operations, without the help of an additional shovel. And like the earlier Marion designs, many were bound for the coal-mining region of southeastern Kansas, including the first 150-B and 175-Bs built. The race to build the largest stripping shovel was officially on between Bucyrus and Marion. The winner was not declared until decades later.

The years leading up to, during, and immediately after World War II saw an increased demand for coal to power the nation's steel plants, railroads, and factories. As larger quantities of coal

were needed, so too were shovels that could get at it. The deeper the coal, the bigger the stripping shovel. In 1914, Bucyrus introduced its very popular 225-B. With a working weight of 348 tons and a 6-cubic-yard dipper on a 75-foot boom, it was more than a match for Marion's Model 271. As with many of the previous strippers of the day, the first 225-B went to work in Kansas. Purchased by the Carney-Cherokee Coal Company of Mulberry, it was the first in a long line of 225-Bs built by Bucyrus. When production ended in 1923, 90 of the shovels had been put into service throughout the country. Not only was the 225-B one of the most popular stripping shovels in its day, it also was the first Bucyrus shovel design to be offered with electric power as an alternative to steam in 1917, matching Marion's engineering feat of 1915.

Not to be outdone by its archrival, Marion introduced its Model 300 in 1915 as an alternative choice to Bucyrus' well-received 225-B. The Model 300 was the same capacity as the 225-B, but weighed 350 tons and was equipped with a 90-foot boom. Produced until 1923, a total of 74 would be built.

Bucyrus Erie 750-B

Introduced in 1928, the Bucyrus Erie 750-B had a dipper capacity range from 12 to 24 cubic yards. The 750-B was built in two versions: one without and the other with a counterbalanced hoist. The first of the counterbalanced hoist machines shipped in 1930, and four were factory built. When production ceased in 1940, 14 shovels of both types had been placed into service. Pictured working in September 1959 at Pittsburg and Midway Coal Mining Company's Paradise Mine in Drakesboro, Kentucky, is a 21-cubic-yard 750-B shovel. This machine actually shipped in 1929 equipped with a 16-yard dipper and the standard hoist system. In the 1950s it was rebuilt with a counterbalanced hoist to accommodate the larger-capacity bucket.
Author's collection

Marion 5600

In 1929, Marion built a special, one-of-a-kind stripping shovel for United Electric Coal Companies called the Type 5600. Carrying a 15-cubic-yard dipper, with an overall working weight of 1,550 tons, it made its home at the company's Mine No. 11 in southern Illinois. In 1957 this same shovel was converted into a bucket wheel excavator.
Author's collection

Left: **Bucyrus Erie 950-B**

Bucyrus Erie introduced its 950-B series stripping shovel in 1935. Weighing approximately 1,250 tons, it was equipped with a nominal dipper capacity of 30 cubic yards. It remained in production until 1941, with 10 shovels produced. This 950-B is shown at work in April 1949 for the Little John Coal Company of Victoria, Illinois. It had originally shipped from the factory in October 1936. *Author's collection*

Below: **Bucyrus Erie 1050-B**

This 45-cubic-yard Bucyrus Erie 1050-B was the last unit of that shovel built by the company. It shipped from the plant in January 1960 for its first home at United Electric Coal Companies' Banner Mine in Illinois. In 1982, the shovel went to work for the Freeman United Coal Mining Company at its Industry Mine, located in Industry, Illinois. It is shown at work here in October 1997. *Urs Peyer*

The Model 300 and the Bucyrus 225-B were the first stripping shovels to be equipped with Ward-Leonard electric controls in 1919. The Ward-Leonard system of electric controls allowed driving motors to be operated at a constant torque, regardless of their speed, automatically adjusting them to the resistance. Under heavy loads, the motors would slow down, and under light loads, speed up. The possibility of electric motors overloading and burning themselves out was greatly reduced. Also, the electric slewing (rotating) and hoist motors could act as brakes, turning themselves into generators, which put electrical power back into the machine's system. The Ward-Leonard controls would prove to be the one choice for the majority of all stripping shovel designs.

Marion once again upped the ante in the stripping shovel wars with Bucyrus with its release of the Model 350 in 1923. Equipped with an 8-cubic-yard dipper, a 90-foot boom, and a working weight of 560 tons, it was considered the largest mobile land machine of its day. The Model 350 could be ordered with steam or electric power. Although initially this model was a rail-mounted

Above: **Marion 5560**
Marion's 5560 type was the company's first stripping shovel to feature a counterbalanced hoist featuring a rack-and-pinion design. Built in two series, the first was produced until 1934 and carried a nominal dipper capacity of 18 cubic yards. The second series was equipped with a nominal 32-cubic-yard bucket and was manufactured from 1935 to 1937. In all, five of the first series were built, and four of the second series. *Author's collection*

Left: **Marion 5561 "The Tiger"**
The Marion 5561 introduced in 1940 was the first stripping shovel built by the company to feature the new knee-action-crowd front-end design. This 5561 originally shipped in December 1943 to Hanna Coal Company, a division of Pittsburgh Consolidation Coal Company, better known as CONSOL, in Cadiz, Ohio. Nicknamed "The Tiger," it would eventually be joined by three other 5561 shovels wearing the Hanna logo: "The Green Hornet," "The Wasp," and "The Groundhog." All were originally equipped with 35-cubic-yard dippers, with working weights of approximately 1,788 tons. In later years, all were upgraded to 46-cubic-yard-capacity buckets. *Author's collection*

Bucyrus Erie 550-B

In 1936, Bucyrus Erie introduced a smaller stripping shovel identified as the 550-B. The 550-B weighed 893 tons and was designed to accept bucket capacities in the 11- to 24-cubic-yard range. Only eight had been built by the time production ended in 1954. This 550-B shipped from the factory in May 1949 destined for South America. Equipped with an 11-yard dipper, it was purchased by the Chile Exploration Company for its Chuquicamata mining operation. It is shown here at work in November 1952. *Author's collection*

design, the company started to offer a crawler option to the shovel line in 1925. This was the first time Marion had offered a crawler design on one of its stripping shovels. In all, 47 units of the Model 350 were manufactured until production ended in 1929.

In 1924, Bucyrus released a design, the 320-B, that again would help put the company on a level playing field with Marion. The 320-B was designed as a 7.5-cubic-yard stripper, but later models would hit 8 cubic yards, equal to the Marion Model 350. It was also available as a steam or electric shovel, and as with the big Marion, crawlers were introduced to free the giant shovel from its railroad tracks in 1925. Average working weight for the 320-B was approximately 438 tons. Production would outlast the Marion by one year when the last of 29 Bucyrus 320-B shovels left the plant in 1930.

Though the American manufacturers Marion and Bucyrus dominated the stripping shovel industry, they were not the only companies at the time that offered such machines. Ruston and Hornsby of England produced three models of stripping shovels from 1923 to 1937. The largest of

these was the Ruston 300, introduced in 1924, of which only four were built when production ended in 1930. With a standard dipper capacity of 8 cubic yards and a working weight of 392 tons, it was just a bit smaller than the Bucyrus 320-B. Like its American counterparts, it was available in steam or electric power, as well as rail mounted or with crawler track mountings. The Ruston 300, along with the Bucyrus 320-B and Marion Model 350, would go down in history as the three largest steam shovel designs ever to be put into service.

The use of steam to power a new stripping shovel design was now in the past. Now, only electricity would power the future larger designs of both Bucyrus and Marion.

The next significant stripping shovel releases by Marion and Bucyrus Erie (formerly Bucyrus Company) were their 5480 and 750-B models, respectively. Released in 1927, the Marion 5480 was a 975-ton shovel design, capable of handling a 12- to 16-cubic-yard dipper, depending on the specified boom length. From day one, the 5480 was designed around eight crawler truck assemblies and electric power. Bucyrus Erie countered

Marion 5760 "Mountaineer"
The most famous of all the stripping shovels was without a doubt the Marion 5760 "Mountaineer." Completed in December 1955, it was the first of the so-called "super-strippers." It was equipped with a 65-cubic-yard dipper on a 150-foot boom and tipped the scales at 2,750 tons. The "Mountaineer" is shown at work in late 1956.
Dale Davis collection

the Marion threat with its new 922-ton 750-B stripper. Shipped in January 1928, the 750-B was a very capable machine and a design that laid the groundwork for the next few Bucyrus stripping shovels introduced. The 750-B was rated at 12 to 16 cubic yards, the same as the Marion. Crawler mountings and electric power were also standard fare. Both designs were evenly matched to each other. Sales were also very similar. When production ended on the 5480 in 1932, 11 shovels had been put into service. The 750-B in its original form would call it a day in 1930 with 10 units built.

But that was not the end of the story for the Bucyrus Erie 750-B. In June 1930 the company shipped a special 750-B stripping shovel to Michigan Limestone in Rogers City, Michigan. The design was fitted with a counterbalanced hoist system at the rear of the shovel, the first of its kind for Bucyrus Erie. The hoist design incorporated a movable counterweight enclosed in an elevator-type tower structure attached to the rear of the revolving frame. The counterweight moved up and down in the structure to counteract the weight difference of the shovel as it went through its digging and dumping cycle. This design helped to increase payload capacity, while at the same time, saved energy. This version of the 750-B, sometimes referred to as a Series II, was equipped

Marion 5760 "Mountaineer"
The Marion 5760 "Mountaineer" was built for the Hanna Coal Company, a division of CONSOL. The shovel was officially put to work on January 30, 1956, at the Georgetown No. 12 Mine near Cadiz, Ohio. *Author's collection*

with an 18-cubic-yard dipper, which helped raise the working weight up to 1,000 tons. Though it was in production until 1940, only four of this type were ever manufactured.

The reason so few 750-B II shovels were built had more to do with a larger design also offered by Bucyrus Erie, which was produced at the same time. Referred to as the 950-B, it was the bigger brother of the 750-B II. Weighing 1,250 tons in full operating trim, the 950-B was a 30-cubic-yard shovel that featured the counterbalanced hoist

Marion 5760 "Big Paul"
The second 5760 shovel delivered by Marion was for Peabody Coal's River King Mine near Freeburg, Illinois, in 1957 and was equipped with a 70-cubic-yard dipper on a 140-foot boom. Christened "Big Paul, the King of Spades," it was named after Peabody employee Paul Duensing, who was in charge of the erection of the shovel and not after the mythical lumberjack Paul Bunyan, as many have surmised over the years. In 1964 the shovel was moved to the Peabody Hawthorn Mine near Carlisle, Indiana. *Author's collection*

first seen on the 750-B II. New to this design was a tubular dipper handle, which could rotate slightly to relieve stress, with a rope crowd and a two-piece boom design—all key features that would find their way into future Bucyrus Erie stripping shovel designs. The first 950-B shovel shipped from the South Milwaukee plant in October 1935 to Shasta Coal Corporation in Bicknell, Indiana. In all, 10 of the shovels were built by the time the model line came to an end in 1941.

Marion's answer to the Bucyrus Erie 750-B and 950-B shovels was the 5560. Marion had actually built a larger shovel than any of the Bucyrus machines of the day in the form of the 5600 in 1929. Weighing 1,550 tons, and initially with a 15-cubic-yard bucket, it was a one-of-a-kind design for United Electric Coal Companies for use in one of their coal mines in southern Illinois. The Marion 5560, which came after the

5600, was actually a smaller machine. Released in 1932, the 1,158-ton shovel was able to handle an 18-cubic-yard bucket, the same as the Bucyrus Erie 750-B II. The 5560 could be ordered equipped with a counterbalanced hoist, much like the unit found on the Bucyrus Erie 750-B II, or in the more conventional configuration without it. In fact, the first Marion 5560 shipped in August 1932 to Clemens Coal Company of Pittsburg, Kansas, was a counterbalanced hoist machine. In October 1935, Marion shipped the first example of a far more robust 5560 machine, sometimes referred to as a Series II. This version was specified with a 32-cubic-yard dipper on a boom length of 105.5 feet. The weight of this model was 1,550 tons, the same as the older Marion 5600 design from 1929. Production ended on the 5560 series in 1937, with five of the original type and four of the larger-capacity Series II built.

Bucyrus Erie 1650-B
This Bucyrus Erie 1650-B shovel was built for the Sunnyhill Coal Company of New Lexington, Ohio, in 1958, and was the second 1650-B produced. The Sunnyhill machine was equipped with a 65-cubic-yard dipper on a 135-foot boom. In later years, this same shovel would be moved to Midland Electric Coal Company's Allendale Mine in Illinois.
Bucyrus International

It was not until 1940 that Marion had a successor to the 5560 ready for the coal industry. Identified as the 5561, it would prove to be one of the company's best-selling stripping shovel designs over 10 cubic yards in capacity. The 5561 had a bucket capacity range of 35 to 45 cubic yards, with an average working weight of 1,788 tons. All would feature Marion's new knee-action crowd front end. The knee-action crowd design had the dipper handle attached to a pivoting stiff leg, which resembled a grasshopper's rear leg. In the older shovel designs, the dipper handle was attached to the boom. In this new design, the relocation of the dipper handle removed undue stress from the main boom and also allowed for the design of far lighter boom structures. The rack-and-pinion crowd mechanism, which supplied the necessary digging force for the knee-action design, was mounted in the gantry above the main housing. Locating the mechanism here greatly reduced the swing inertia of the shovel in operation. This crowd design would be the hallmark of all Marion stripping shovels from this time forward.

Marion shipped its first 5561 shovel in March 1940 to the Tecumseh Coal Corporation in

Above: **Bucyrus Erie 1650-B Dipper**
The 65-cubic-yard dipper on Sunnyhill Coal Company's Bucyrus Erie 1650-B was large enough to swallow a fairly large Caterpillar dozer with little trouble, as in this publicity photo taken in November 1958.
Bucyrus International

Right: **Bucyrus Erie 1650-B**
The third 1650-B shovel to be built by Bucyrus Erie was for the United Electric Coal Companies for use at their Fidelity Mine located near Du Quoin, Illinois. Shipped from the factory in August 1961, it officially went to work in March 1962. This particular 1650-B was equipped with a 70-cubic-yard dipper on a 135-foot boom. Fidelity Mine's 1650-B is shown hard at work here in March 1962. *Bucyrus International*

Dickeyville, Indiana, equipped with a 35-cubic-yard dipper. After a short stay at this mine, it was moved to Peabody Coal Company's Rogers County No. 2 Mine in Vinita, Oklahoma. In all, 17 of the 5561 strippers were put into service, with the last leaving the Marion plant in June 1956. It is interesting to note that Peabody Coal took one of its 5561 shovels (the second unit shipped in December 1941) and four of its older 5560 machines and built a one-of-a-kind stripping shovel identified as a Peabody Type 5562P for its Bee Veer Mine in Macon, Missouri. Eventually, this hybrid was moved to the company's Rogers County No. 1 Mine. No records exist as to the exact specifications of this unique Type 5562 stripping shovel.

As the technology of the day made the stripping shovels larger and more productive, there still was a market for machines of this type of a slightly smaller size. Both Marion and Bucyrus Erie produced smaller stripping shovels that benefited from the technological advances that first found their home in the larger machines. In 1936, Bucyrus Erie released its 893-ton 550-B, which could be equipped with an 11- to 24-cubic-yard dipper. Marion countered this in 1941 with the 1,033-ton 5323. The 5323 usually had dipper capacities ranging from 11 to 20 cubic yards. The Bucyrus Erie 550-B benefited from a two-piece boom design, a round tubular dipper handle, and rear-mounted counterbalanced hoist, just like its big brothers. The Marion 5323 also shared features that were found on the company's larger machines, such as the new knee-action crowd front end. Bucyrus Erie shipped its first 550-B, a 16-cubic-yard machine, in August 1936, and the last, a 20-cubic-yard version in September 1954.

Bucyrus Erie 1650-B "Mr. Dillon"
Last of the 1650-B shovels to be placed into service by Bucyrus Erie was the Green Coal Company's machine for their Panther Mine located near Owensboro, Kentucky. The shovel officially went on line in March 1965 equipped with a 70-cubic-yard dipper on a 135-foot boom. Working weight was right around 2,874 tons. Panther Mine personnel named their large stripping machines after characters from the popular television series *Gunsmoke*. Pictured in January 1972 is "Mr. Dillon" keeping the peace at the Panther Mine. *Author's collection*

In all, eight of the shovels were manufactured. As for the Marion 5323, it would end its production run in 1961, with a total of nine units shipped.

Continuing on with the "bigger is better" philosophy, Bucyrus Erie introduced a successor to its popular 950-B in the form of the 1050-B. The 1050-B was Bucyrus Erie's counterpart to Marion's 5561 shovel offering. Weighing 1,535 tons, the 1050-B was just a little lighter than the 5561. Bucket capacities for the big stripper ranged from 26 to 45 cubic yards. All of the major design features on the Bucyrus Erie 950-B were also present on the 1050-B, including the counterweight hoist. The first 1050-B was shipped in December 1941 to the Fairview Collieries Corporation's Flamingo Mine in Fairview, Illinois, and was equipped with a 33-cubic-yard dipper.

Marion 5761

This aerial view taken around 1980 is of a Marion 5761 working at Peabody Coal's Gibraltar Mine near Central City, Kentucky. Originally shipped in April 1968, it was the 12th out of 15 Marion 5761 shovels to be built. The last officially shipped from the Marion factory on December 31, 1970. Sadly, in February 1984 the Gibraltar 5761 was lost in a freak accident at the mine, when the shovel tipped over as it was being moved to a new pit location. *Peabody Energy*

Marion 5761 "Stripmaster"

Peabody Coal Company purchased the first Marion 5761 built. Shipped from the factory to Peabody's Lynnville Mine in southern Indiana in September 1959, it carried a 65-cubic-yard dipper on a 165-foot boom. Operating weight was in the neighborhood of 3,788 tons. Christened the "Stripmaster," it would spend its entire working life at the Lynnville operations. It is shown here at work in 1977. *Author's collection*

After a few years of operation at this mine, the shovel was moved to Midland Coal Company's Elm Mine, located near Trivoli, Illinois. In all, 12 of the 1050-B shovels were put into service at coal mines throughout the Midwest, with the largest machine populations located in Kentucky and Illinois. The last of the 1050-Bs was a 45-cubic-yard machine, the largest bucket capacity of the group, which shipped in January 1960. Destined for United Electric Coal Companies' Banner Mine in Illinois, it would prove to be the best of the 1050-Bs, if for no other reason than its longevity in active mining duty. In 1982, the shovel was moved to Freeman United Coal Mining Company's new Industry Mine, located in Industry, Illinois. There it has worked for the last 20 years with little downtime. Though it seemed on more than a few occasions that that shovel's time on this earth was over, the mine was able to get new coal contracts, which kept the miners, as well as their shovel, at

work. At the time of this writing, the last of the 1050-Bs still has a few more years left in it.

Working in tandem with the last 1050-B shovel is a large Kolbe/Bucyrus Erie W3A Wheel Excavator. What makes this bucket wheel so unique is that its lower works is actually made up from the first 1050-B built. This unit was purchased and moved up from Midland Coal in 1981. So, not only does the Industry Mine own the last 1050-B stripper, it also has the first, if only as part of another machine. As long as the Industry Mine remains in operation, so will the 1050-B shovel and W3A wheel.

After the releases of the Marion 5561 and Bucyrus Erie 1050-B stripping shovel types, the rivalry between the two companies concerning who would field the next machine took some time off. During this time period, the marketplace seemed perfectly happy with the sized shovels they already had at their disposal. That ended in

Marion 5761
This view of the Marion 5761 at Peabody Coal's Alston Mine in Kentucky, taken around 1980, shows the type of activity surrounding one of these "super-strippers" during maintenance. When a shovel such as this was shut down, it was the mine's top priority to get it back on line as soon as possible. The Alston shovel was equipped with a 75-cubic-yard dipper and was the ninth 5761 shipped. *Peabody Energy*

Bucyrus Erie 3850-B Lot I "Big Hog"

The Bucyrus Erie 3850-B Lot I shovel was a true engineering marvel for its time. Weighing approximately 9,000 tons, the 3850-B Lot I was the world's largest mobile land machine in its day. It was built for Peabody Coal Company for use at its Sinclair Mine located near Drakesboro, Kentucky. Pictured in August 1962 is the first 3850-B as it gets ready to leave the erection site on its 3-mile journey to the mine pit. *Author's collection*

1956, when the Hanna Coal Company, a division of Pittsburgh Consolidation Coal Company (CONSOL), dedicated the mining industry's next biggest release, the Mountaineer.

Hanna had already been operating four Marion 5561 shovels at its various mining sites around Cadiz, Ohio. To meet future mining requirements of the company, a much larger shovel was going to be needed. Marion engineers' answer to Hanna's requests was the 5760 type, by far the largest stripping shovel ever to be manufactured up until that time. Weighing 2,750 tons, it was a giant among giants in its day. It was also the first of the so-called "super-strippers." Stripping shovels were large, but super-strippers were larger still. Because of the size of the shovel

Right: **Bucyrus Erie 3850-B Lot I "Big Hog"**

The Bucyrus Erie 3850-B Lot I shovel, nicknamed "Big Hog" by the Sinclair Mine's employees, was equipped with a huge 115-cubic-yard dipper which, when attached to the 134-foot dipper handle, measured 180 feet long. Payload capacity was approximately 175 tons. *Author's collection*

design, Hanna early on christened the shovel "The Mountaineer," which was painted on the sides and back of the machine. On-site assembly of the Mountaineer commenced in June 1955 and was completed by late December. On January 19, 1956, the Mountaineer was officially dedicated at a special event held at the shovel's erection site for members of the mining industry, as well as the local press and TV crews. After the event, the shovel started to make its way down to the working pit of the Georgetown No. 12 Mine. On January 30, the shovel was officially put to work.

The Mountaineer employed Marion's knee-action crowd front end, as well as dual operator's cabs and a three-person elevator that ran right through the center pin of the shovel, a first for a stripping shovel. The first 5760 carried a 65-cubic-yard bucket, suspended from a 150-foot boom. The shovel would eventually utilize two bucket types, one with a flat bottom and the other with a rounded lip and bottom, both rated at 65 cubic yards with 100-ton payloads. After a long trial period, it was found that the rounded bottom design was far superior to the flat bottom.

Bucyrus Erie 3850-B Lot I "Big Hog"

"Big Hog" was the centerpiece of the Peabody Sinclair mining operations. With its 210-foot boom and 180-foot dipper handle, the shovel had an impressive working radius, capable of digging in one spot and depositing it 420 feet away. Here is "Big Hog" doing just that in January 1983. *Author's collection*

Bucyrus Erie 3850-B Lot II
The Peabody River King 3850-B was slowly moved out of its old pit onto the surface for its trek to its new location. This process of moving a stripping shovel is often referred to as a "deadhead." The giant 9,350-ton shovel was supported by approximately 200 oak mats, each costing $1,100. These were necessary to support the weight of the shovel and reduce the overall ground pressure exerted and provide a stable surface for it to travel on. *Randall Hyman*

Bucyrus Erie 3850-B Lot II
In 1988 it was necessary for Peabody to move its massive Bucyrus Erie 3850-B Lot II shovel to a new pit location at the River King No. 6 Mine. Starting on August 15 and ending on August 19, the shovel was moved a total of 1 mile to its new mining location. *Randall Hyman*

For the most part, the Mountaineer operated with the rounded version. Early on in the shovel's life, many reports had the capacity of it listed at 60 cubic yards. In fact, the Mountaineer from day one was equipped with a 65-cubic-yard dipper. It turned out the 60-cubic-yard number was related to union issues and not a typographical error as many had surmised.

Other than a boom collapse on January 26, 1971, due to part of the highwall collapsing and overloading the dipper, the Mountaineer was one of the company's most reliable shovels. For most in the industry, it is considered the most famous shovel of all, thanks in part to its catchy name.

Following in the Mountaineer's footsteps, Marion went on to build four more 5760-type strippers. In April 1957, Marion shipped the second 5760 shovel to Peabody Coal's River King Mine near Freeburg, Illinois. This unit actually carried a larger 70-cubic-yard bucket, but had a slightly shorter 140-foot boom. Not to be outdone by Hanna when it came to names, Peabody christened its 5760 "Big Paul, the King of Spades." Production ended on the 5760 after the fifth unit shipped in April 1958.

Marion's 5760 Mountaineer may have intimidated many who saw it, but not the engineers at Bucyrus Erie, who before long designed a super-

stripping shovel to rival Marion's, best known as the 1650-B. The 1650-B design did away with the counterbalanced hoist system of the previous Bucyrus Erie shovel designs. The 1650-B shovels also featured an operator's cab whose design offered a panoramic view of the work area. This cab design was unique to the 1650-B series and is considered the nicest looking of all the super-strippers.

The first 1650-B ordered was manufactured for Peabody Coal for its River Queen Mine near Central City, Kentucky. Shipping in November 1956, the first unit was up and digging by April 1957. The River Queen shovel was specified with a 55-cubic-yard dipper on a 145-foot boom. Operating weight was right around 2,450 tons. This particular 1650-B was quite active and actually worked at four different mining sites in its lifetime. After a

stay at the River Queen Mine, it was shipped to the Vogue Mine. From there it was off to the Riverview Mine. After a few more years of service, it was barged up the Green River to Green Coal's Henderson County Mine Number 1 in Kentucky, where it would spend the rest of its working life well into the early 1990s.

In all, five Bucyrus Erie 1650-B super-strippers eventually were built, with the last shipping in August 1964 to Green Coal's Panther Mine near Owensboro, Kentucky. This unit was equipped with a 70-cubic-yard bucket, a 135-foot boom, and weighed 2,874 tons, far more than the original 55-cubic-yard unit. The 1650-B never received much notoriety during its production. Even though the series was a match to Marion's first super-stripping shovel, it just never captured the public's imagination like the Mountaineer had.

Bucyrus Erie 3850-B Lot II
As the 3850-B shovel moved along, the oak mats were taken up from behind it and replaced in the front. This process was repeated for the next mile until the shovel reached the new pit location. During the move, the shovel passed through a levee, across a creek, under a power line, and over a township roadway. The move of the 3850-B went through with no damage sustained by the shovel or its surrounding areas.
Randall Hyman

Bucyrus Erie 1850-B "Brutus"

The Bucyrus Erie 1850-B manufactured for the Pittsburg and Midway Coal Mining Company (P&M) was another one of the builder's more renowned stripping shovels. Named "Brutus" by the mine's superintendent, Emil Sandeen, the 90-cubic-yard shovel officially started working in June 1963. *Bucyrus International*

But all five of the 1650-B shovels were exemplary designs, with long and productive working lives in Kentucky, Ohio, and Illinois.

In 1959, Marion introduced an improved version of its 5760 super-stripper in the form of the 5761. The 5761 was Marion's response to Bucyrus Erie's 1650-B stripper, and was, in fact, the best-selling super-stripper to be produced by either company. The 5761 looked much like the 5760 series, but had a bucket capacity range of 60 to 75 cubic yards, with an average working weight of 3,788 tons. The first 5761 shipped from Marion in September 1959 destined for Peabody Coal's Lynnville Mine and was referred to as the "Stripmaster." The Stripmaster was specified with

Bucyrus Erie 1850-B "Brutus"

The 1850-B spent its entire working life operating at P&M's Mine 19 in Hallowell, Kansas. The shovel stood approximately 16 stories tall and carried a 150-foot boom. Working weight was around 5,225 tons. In April 1974, "Brutus" was parked after the mine was closed. Only one Bucyrus Erie 1850-B was ever built, and it's shown here in June 1963. *Bucyrus International*

a 65-cubic-yard dipper and a 165-foot boom. In January 1968, Marion shipped its first 5761 equipped with rope crowd to Ayrshire Collieries Corporation's Wright Mine, near Boonville, Indiana. This unit was also the first of any of the company's super-strippers to be commissioned with rope crowd. The last 5761 built left the factory in December 1970, destined for Arch Mineral's Fabius Mine in Alabama. In all, 15 stripping shovels and 1 crawler base were manufactured. The crawler base was built for Peabody Coal to support a Krupp bucket wheel excavator ordered for its Northern Illinois Mine near Mullins.

Super-strippers took a gigantic leap in size in 1962 with the commissioning of Bucyrus Erie's 3850-B series. Built to order for Peabody Coal, it was truly an engineering marvel for its day. The 3850-B was simply huge. Weighing approximately 9,000 tons, it was more than three times the size of the mighty Mountaineer. The shovel was a true leviathan on land. Towering some 20 stories into the air, it was the world's largest land machine for its day, if only for a short while. The 3850-B was dedicated into service in August 1962 at Peabody's Sinclair Mine near Drakesboro, Kentucky, after an 11-month field assembly time.

Marion 6360 "The Captain"
In 1965, Marion introduced its monstrous 6360 stripping shovel. With its 180-cubic-yard dipper, it was the world's largest excavator for its day. Built for Southwestern Illinois Coal Corporation for use at its Captain Mine, located near Percy, Illinois, it is shown here in October 1965 in its original beige-and-maroon color scheme. *Author's collection*

Marion 6360 "The Captain"
Christened "The Captain," the Marion 6360 was repainted white and blue after the Arch Mineral Corporation purchased the Captain Mine in 1973. Though the operating weight of the 6360 was originally stated as 14,000 tons, its true weight after assembly was closer to 15,000 tons, a world record for a mobile land machine. Here is the Captain at work in September 1983. *Peter N. Grimshaw*

Christened "Big Hog" by the mine's workers, the giant stripper wielded a 115-cubic-yard dipper, capable of holding 175 tons of material. The shovel's boom length was 210 feet, with a 180-degree working radius of 420 feet at maximum bucket height. It would work continuously at the Sinclair operations until the mine was shut down in November 1985.

Peabody Coal would also order another Bucyrus Erie 3850-B super-stripper for use at its River King Mine No. 6, located near Freeburg, Illinois. The second unit, referred to as 3850-B Lot II, was different in a few key areas when compared to the first 3850-B Lot I shovel. Most significant for the Lot II shovel was its larger 140-cubic-yard dipper, capable of holding 210 tons of overburden. To make this possible, the boom of the Lot II

Above:

Marion 6360 "The Captain"
The Marion 6360 shovel was simply huge. With its 215-foot boom, 133-foot dipper handle, dual-gantry-supported rack-and-pinion-driven crowd, and knee-action front end, the 6360 was designed to uncover two seams of coal simultaneously. The shovel also had a 16-foot clearance under it to allow vehicles to pass safely beneath it between the crawlers.
Peter N. Grimshaw

Right: **Marion 5860**
Marion only produced two 5860 stripping shovels, both for the Truax-Traer Coal Company, a division of CONSOL. Each 5860 carried an 80-cubic-yard dipper on a 180-foot boom. Average working weight was 5,175 tons each. The first shovel was delivered to Truax-Traer's Red Ember Mine near Fiatt, Illinois, in 1965. The second machine, pictured, worked at its Burning Star No. 3 Mine, located near Sparta, Illinois, starting in 1966.
Author's collection

machine was slightly shorter at 200 feet in length. But overall working weight was up compared to the Lot I shovel, with the second unit coming in at 9,350 tons, a new world record. Officially dedicated into service on August 13, 1964, the Lot II shovel would spend its entire working life at the River King No. 6 operation, until it was decommissioned in September 1992. In all, only two of the 3850-B series shovels were built by Bucyrus Erie, with the Lot II machine holding the honors of the largest shovel ever to be assembled by the company.

During the fabrication of the second 3850-B at Bucyrus Erie's South Milwaukee shops, the company was also in the process of building another super-stripper called the 1850-B. Though not on the same scale as the 140-cubic-yard machine, the 1850-B was nonetheless a very large shovel. Weighing 5,225 tons, with a 90-cubic-yard dipper on a 150-foot boom, the shovel was custom built for Pittsburg and Midway Coal Mining Company (P&M) for use at its Mine 19 in Hallowell, Kansas. Nicknamed "Brutus," it officially went to work in May 1963. Brutus was an aesthetically attractive shovel design. Painted in P&M's corporate colors of orange and black, the

Above right: **Bucyrus Erie 1950-B "Silver Spade"**
Another one of Bucyrus Erie's more famous stripping shovels was its first 1950-B, known as "The Silver Spade." The "Spade" was named in recognition of the 25th anniversary of Hanna Coal Company, a division of the CONSOL group. It was also Bucyrus Erie's first stripping shovel to feature the knee-action crowd front end, originally pioneered by Marion. The 7,200-ton shovel is shown here getting ready to go to work in late November 1965, near Cadiz, Ohio.
Author's collection

Right: **Marion 6360 "The Captain"**
The massive bucket on the Marion 6360 was rated at 180 cubic yards, which translated to a 270-ton payload. The dipper alone weighed 165 tons empty! It was also equipped with dual doors that helped reduce the shock impact on the dipper structure as they slammed shut after dumping. Each of the four crawler assemblies was steered by means of a single, massive hydraulic cylinder operating at a pressure of 5,000 pounds per square inch, one per assembly, and were mounted high enough to allow vehicles to pass underneath.
Author's collection

Above: **Bucyrus Erie 1950-B "Silver Spade"**
Though the Silver Spade's 105-cubic-yard dipper might not have been the largest in the industry at the time, it was still considered quite massive. As one can clearly see, the bucket is capable of swallowing not only the service truck parked next to it, but another one as well. *Bucyrus International*

Right: **Bucyrus Erie 1950-B "Silver Spade" Dipper**
The dipper of the 1950-B "Silver Spade" was rated at 105 cubic yards in capacity, with a payload of approximately 160 tons. Like its name suggested, the shovel's dipper was painted silver when new. *Author's collection*

1850-B was eye-catching, at least as far as a stripping shovel was concerned. But looks aren't everything in the mining business. After only 11 years of operation, the one-of-a-kind shovel was parked when Mine 19 was closed. That was not the end of Brutus, however, as will be explained in more detail in chapter 5.

The year 1965 was busy for Marion. The company had not one, but two new super-stripper designs ready for release. One of these was the 5860 type, which was in the same size class as Bucyrus Erie's 1850-B. The other Marion design was the 6360. To say the 6360 was Marion's answer to Bucyrus Erie's 3850-B Lot II shovel was really an understatement. The 6360 was simply the largest mobile land machine, shovel or otherwise, to ever crawl across the face of the earth. Period.

The Marion 6360 was built for Southwestern Illinois Coal Corporation, for use at its new Captain Mine, located near Percy, Illinois. The 6360 was designed to uncover two coal seams simultaneously during operations utilizing a 180-

cubic-yard dipper, the largest ever fabricated for a shovel. The payload capacity of this bucket was a staggering 270 tons. The dipper alone weighed 165 tons empty. From it massive dual gantry design, to each of its eight 45-foot-long, 16-foot-high, gigantic crawler trucks, there was nothing small in stature on the 6360. Initially, the mightiest of the super-strippers had a calculated working weight of approximately 14,000 tons. But design changes made to the shovel after it went to work, including a redesign of the bucket itself, raised its weight to 15,000 tons, the most for any type of mobile land machine, a record which still stands even to this day.

On October 15, 1965, the most powerful shovel of them all was dedicated into active service at the Captain Mine. Christened "The Captain," it was named after Thomas C. Mullins. Referred to as "Captain Mullins" by everyone who knew him, he was a leader in the development of strip-mining coal technology in the early 20th century. The Marion 6360, as well as the mine itself, was named after Captain Mullins by his son, Bill Mullins, who was the principal founder of the Captain Mine.

In its original form, the Captain shovel was painted beige and maroon, the corporate colors of Southwestern Illinois Coal. But after the mining

Bucyrus Erie 1950-B "Silver Spade"
The Silver Spade was equipped with a 200-foot boom and 122-foot dipper handle, giving the shovel an impressive working range. This shovel's sister machine, "The GEM of Egypt," was configured with a 170-foot boom and 102-foot dipper handle. This aerial view of the "Spade" was taken in August 1968. *Bucyrus International*

Bucyrus Erie 1950-B "Silver Spade"
In 2003 the "Silver Spade" is the only super-stripper still in operation today. It is shown here working at CONSOL's Mahoning Valley Mine No. 36, located near Cadiz, Ohio, in May 1994. It would be temporarily parked in November 1995 and then reactivated in July 1997. *ECO*

THE GEM OF EGYPT

operation was sold to Arch Mineral Corporation in 1973, it was repainted white and blue. It stayed that way until the late 1980s, when it received a fresh coat of white and blue paint, with the addition of a red stripe—a paint scheme which lasted until the shovel ceased operations in 1991. Only one 6360 type was ever constructed.

While the 6360 was grabbing all of the headlines, Marion had quietly put two 5860-type shovels into service. Both of these machines carried the same specifications: 80-cubic-yard dippers, 180-foot booms, and approximate working weights of 5,175 tons. Both shovels were also purchased by CONSOL's Truax-Traer Coal Company. The first unit started operations in June 1965 at the Red Ember Mine near Fiatt, Illinois. The second went on line in July 1966 at the

Burning Star No. 3 Mine near Sparta, Illinois. This second shovel would eventually go on to bigger and better things in the early 1980s after it was sold to Arch of Illinois. In 1985, the shovel was rebuilt into a base for a massive cross-pit bucket wheel excavator called the 5872-WX. Engineered by Bucyrus Erie, the bucket wheel structure was mounted on top of the main housing of the Marion 5860. The 5872-WX started work at the Captain mining operation in February 1986.

While 1965 certainly was a banner year for Marion when it came to its super-stripping shovel program, it was also quite memorable for Bucyrus Erie as well. In November 1965, just a few weeks after the Marion 6360 went on line, Bucyrus Erie dedicated its first 1950-B super-stripper into service at CONSOL's mining operations located

Bucyrus Erie 1950-B
"The GEM of Egypt"
Bucyrus Erie manufactured only two 1950-B stripping shovels. The second of these, "The GEM of Egypt," was dedicated into service in January 1967. Built for CONSOL's Hanna Coal Company for use at its Egypt Valley Mine, located near Barnesville, Ohio, the 6,850-ton "GEM" carried a 130-cubic-yard dipper capable of handling a 200-ton payload, on a 170-foot boom. It is shown at work here in November 1967.
Bucyrus International

Marion 5960 "Big Digger"
Peabody's Marion 5960 carried its 125-cubic-yard bucket on a dipper handle measuring 131 feet in length, including bucket. The main boom was 215 feet in length. The 5960, nicknamed "Big Digger," also featured the same type of hydraulic-cylinder steering of the crawler assemblies originally introduced on the mammoth 6360 shovel. Here the "Big Digger" is getting ready to take another dipper-full in early 1977.
Author's collection

near Cadiz, Ohio. Christened the "Silver Spade," it was named to commemorate the 25th anniversary of the Hanna Coal Company, a subsidiary of CONSOL. The Silver Spade was equipped with a 105-cubic-yard dipper suspended from a 200-foot-long boom. Its working weight was 7,200 tons. Unique to a Bucyrus Erie stripper was its use of a knee-action crowd and one-piece boom design. This was made possible with a joint agreement made between Bucyrus Erie and Marion concern-

ing some of their patented stripping shovel engineering designs. CONSOL had requested that the Bucyrus Erie design use the knee-action front end favored by Marion. To make the Silver Spade a reality, Bucyrus Erie offered Marion the use of its rope crowd technology, in return for use of its knee-action front-end design. In the end, Bucyrus Erie got its new front end to replace its two-piece boom design, and Marion got rope crowd technology to replace its own rack-and-pinion crowd systems. This arrangement led to some of the most advanced stripping shovel designs ever to be built by either firm.

In February 1967, Bucyrus Erie put its second 1950-B to work for CONSOL at its Hanna Coal Company's Egypt Valley Mine site, located in Barnesville, Ohio. Referred to as "The GEM of Egypt" (GEM stood for Giant Excavating Machine), it differed from the Silver Spade in two key areas: The GEM of Egypt was specified with a 130-cubic-yard dipper, capable of handling a 200-ton payload. To accommodate the larger bucket, the boom was 30 feet shorter in length to Spade's boom, with GEM's coming in at 170 feet. Other than that, the GEM featured the same knee-action front end with rope crowd found on the Silver Spade. Approximate working weight of the GEM was 6,850 tons, but in most news releases, that figure was simply rounded out to 7,000 tons. The 1950-B GEM would be the last stripping shovel to be manufactured by Bucyrus Erie.

The last two Marion designs of super-stripping shovels were the 5900 and 5960. Both of these designs were similar in execution. Both

Above: **Marion 5960 "Big Digger"**
The second-largest stripping shovel to be built by Marion was its 5960. Placed into service around September 1969 at Peabody Coal's River Queen Mine near Greenville, Kentucky, it was equipped with a 125-cubic-yard dipper. Overall working weight of the shovel was 9,338 tons. Only one 5960 was ever built. *Peabody Energy*

Marion 5900
Marion built only two 5900 series stripping shovels, the first of which shipped to Peabody Coal's Lynnville Mine, located near Lynnville, Indiana, in July 1968. It was officially dedicated into service in November of that year. The Peabody 5900 was equipped with a 105-cubic-yard dipper on a 200-foot boom. *Peabody Energy*

Marion 5900

Peabody's Marion 5900 was the principal stripping machine at its Lynnville mining operations. Weighing 6,925 tons, the 5900 was about the size of a Bucyrus Erie 1950-B shovel type. Here the 5900 is doing what it did best, uncovering rich coal seams in May 1999. *ECO*

featured rope crowd in conjunction with the knee-action front end. And the first of both machine types were to be purchased by Peabody Coal. The first 5900 was placed into service in November 1968 at Peabody's Lynnville Mine in Indiana. This particular shovel was originally equipped with a 105-cubic-yard dipper on a 200-foot boom and had a working weight of some 6,925 tons. The 5960 made its home at Peabody's River Queen Mine in Kentucky. Nicknamed the "Big Digger," the 5960 was specified with a 125-cubic-yard dipper, the second largest carried by a Marion shovel. Its boom length was 215 feet, with

a working weight of 9,338 tons. It started operations around September 1969 as the fourth-largest-capacity shovel in the world. With respect to weight, it was the third heaviest, just a few tons behind the second-place Bucyrus Erie 3850-B Lot II machine.

On April 30, 1971, Marion Power Shovel officially shipped its last stripping shovel, super or otherwise, a Type 5900. The second 5900 was similar to the first Peabody machine from 1968, but there were differences: this 7,250-ton 5900 was configured to uncover two coal seams at the same time. To make this possible, the shovel was equipped with a taller gantry and a 210-foot boom. It was also the first stripping shovel to be equipped with a variable-pitch bucket. The bucket was hinged at its mounting points on the dipper handle, which allowed it to rotate under load. This kept it flat on the pit floor while it began to fill and provided a better cutting action on the working face of the highwall. Not long after the commissioning, the first 5900 was retrofitted with this type of variable-pitch bucket design as well. The second 5900 started working operations in October 1971 at AMAX's Leahy Mine, which was just across the street from the Captain Mine. The last 5900 worked at this site until March 1986, when it and the mine property itself were purchased by Arch of Illinois. The shovel was eventually moved into pit operations adjacent to the 6360. The 5900 was originally painted in AMAX red and white colors, but in August 1992 the shovel was repainted in the Arch red-white-and-blue corporate motif.

The end of the stripping shovel era came not with a bang but a whimper. Actually, it was Marion and Bucyrus Erie that contributed to its demise by producing a competing stripping machine, referred to as a walking dragline, which will be explained in greater detail in chapter 5.

Above: **Marion 5900**
The Marion 5900 at Peabody's Lynnville Mine featured the knee-action front end and rope crowd. The second 5900, built in 1971 by Marion for AMAX Coal Company's Leahy Mine near Percy, Illinois, was equipped with a taller gantry than that found on the Peabody machine, as well as a longer 210-foot boom. It also weighed a bit more at 7,250 tons. The image shown is of the Peabody 5900 in May 1995. *ECO*

Left: **Marion 5900 Crawlers**
The Marion 5900 was supported by eight massive crawler assemblies. Each of these sections was 34 feet long. Width of the entire truck was 21 feet. The width of each track belt was 82 inches. *ECO*

Marion 5900 Operator's Cab

The vantage point from the operator's cab of the 5900 gave a clear view of the digging area. All of the shovel's major digging functions were controlled by two hand levers and two foot pedals. The hand levers controlled the hoist and crowd functions, while the foot pedals controlled the swinging and stopping of the upper works. All controls were electric in nature. *ECO*

Marion 5900

In the early 1980s, the Peabody Marion 5900 was retrofitted with a variable-pitch dipper. The hinged design of this bucket allowed it to rotate slightly under load, allowing for a better fill. This design was first used on the AMAX 5900 shovel in 1971. Stripping shovels the size of the 5900 usually had a rubber-tired wheel dozer of some kind dedicated to it. Their speed made them the perfect pit cleanup tool while the shovel was in operation. *ECO*

Marion 5900

In a surface mining operation, there is nothing more majestic than a shovel standing tall with its dipper held high. In the not-too-distant future, this site will vanish from the countryside forever, as the mighty stripping shovels go the way of the dinosaurs. This is the Peabody Lynnville Marion 5900 in 1999, its last year of operation. *ECO*

Chapter Three

LOADING SHOVELS

As the steam vapors began to dissipate during the early 1920s, gasoline-, diesel-, and electric-powered cable-loading shovels of the tracked variety soon rendered the railroad shovel concept obsolete. Shovel manufacturers were all too eager to dispense with steam-powered designs to make room for the faster and more efficient machines that the marketplace was demanding. Though not as large or heavy as the stripping shovels, the cable-loading shovels were just as important, if not more so, than the giant strippers. Each had its role to play and a job to do.

The loading shovel was the principal excavating tool for the small contractor, road builder, developer, and miner. From the 1910s through the early 1960s, the cable shovel was the principal means of digging and loading earth. One must remember that during this time period, there was really no other means to do this type of work. Front-end, rubber-tired wheel loaders did not start to find favor in the earthmoving industry until the mid-1950s. The 1960s saw the acceptance of hydraulic machines as an alternative to cable-type shovels. In the mining industry, cable shovels have been, and are presently, the machine of choice for large-scale operations worldwide. During the heyday of the cable shovel, literally hundreds of companies worldwide built these machines. Many of these shovel types could also be configured as cable backhoes, draglines, and cranes. In North America, companies such as Insley, Koehring, Lorain, and Manitowoc, all built popular cable shovels that were well suited for contractor use. For larger quarry and mining operations, however, the manufacturing firms of Northwest, Lima, Bucyrus Erie, Marion, and P&H produced the bulk of the shovels used in these industries. In particular, the last three companies mentioned went on to dominate the mining industry with cable shovel model offerings that could not be matched, let alone produced, by any other manufacturer.

As steam power faded, so did many of the companies whose principal business was the production of this type of earthmover. Though many disappeared altogether, some were able to adapt to the changing marketplace and continue on. For some firms, survival required merging with existing companies. For others, being purchased outright by a larger manufacturer was the only means for survival. No one benefited more from this industry upheaval than Bucyrus and Marion. During the first half of the 20th century, both companies grew and expanded through the mergers and acquisitions of competing and allied equipment manufacturers. And both firms were the better because of it.

Bucyrus Erie 295-B
The 295-B was another one of Bucyrus Erie's all-time great electric mining shovel series. Launched in 1972, the 27-cubic-yard 295-B formed the loading backbone for many mining operations around the world. Weighing 670 tons, it was in direct competition with Marion's 201-M mining shovel from 1975. Pictured in October 1995 is a 295-B loading a 240-ton-capacity Caterpillar 793B hauler at the AMAX Eagle Butte Mine, located just north of Gillette, Wyoming. Today, this mine is operated by RAG Coal West. *ECO*

P&H 1200WL

P&H built its first two construction and mining shovel models equipped with Ward-Leonard electric controls in 1932, the 1200WL and the 1400WL. The 4-cubic-yard 1400WL was placed into service on August 19, 1932, but for whatever reason, the 2-cubic-yard 1200WL did not ship from P&H until 1933. Production ended on the 1200WL in 1935, with the 1400WL lasting until 1941. Pictured is the first 1200WL undergoing testing at P&H's proving grounds in Milwaukee, Wisconsin. *Keith Haddock collection*

After The Bucyrus Company purchased the Vulcan Steam Shovel Company in 1910 to form Bucyrus-Vulcan (merged into Bucyrus Company in 1911), the company went on to add still more firms to round out its product lines. In 1927, Bucyrus Company became Bucyrus Erie, after it merged with the Erie Steam Shovel Company. Bucyrus Erie went on to establish Ruston-Bucyrus, Ltd. in Lincoln, England, which was co-owned by Bucyrus Erie and Ruston and Hornsby, Ltd. Then in 1931, Bucyrus Erie acquired interest in the Monighan Manufacturing Company of Chicago, Illinois, builders of dragline-type excavators. This new company entity was referred to as Bucyrus-Monighan. But as with previous dual-named mergers from the company's past, it would be merged with the parent Bucyrus Erie firm in 1946. All of these corporate maneuvers gave Bucyrus Erie the wherewithal to compete, and in some cases dominate, various areas of the construction and earthmoving marketplace.

While Bucyrus Erie was investing in its future, the Marion Steam Shovel Company was also making some moves of its own. In 1946, it changed its name to the Marion Power Shovel Company, to better reflect the types of machines it was building. To expand its contractor-sized shovel and dragline offerings, Marion purchased the Osgood Company of Marion, Ohio, in 1954. In 1961, Marion added the Quick Way Truck Shovel Company of Denver, Colorado, to its holdings. It was set up as a separate division of Marion called the Quick-Way Crane Shovel Company. The smaller Quick-Way machines were marketed through Marion dealerships to complement the company's larger excavator offerings. During this time period, Marion was able to counter almost every model line put forth by Bucyrus

Erie when it came to excavators, cranes, and drills. It was a legendary competitive corporate battle, not unlike that of "Ford versus Chevy," but this time it was in the earthmoving business as opposed to the automotive industry.

Though Bucyrus Erie and Marion were some of the largest corporate entities in the fabrication of quarry and mining shovels, there were others that also played key roles in these industries as well. Companies such as P&H Harnischfeger, Northwest Engineering, and Lima, would all field large excavator types that would go head to head with the best from both Bucyrus Erie and Marion.

P&H can trace its ancestry back to 1884, when Alonzo Pawling and Henry Harnischfeger formed the company Pawling and Harnischfeger, Engineering and Machinists. Located in Milwaukee, Wisconsin, the company manufactured knitting and sewing machines. By 1888, the firm began producing electric overhead cranes in quantity. In 1910, the company introduced a vertical ladder-type trenching machine. This was the company's first

The years 1932, 1934, and 1935 were pivotal in engineering design for P&H. In 1932, the company built its first Ward-Leonard-controlled electric-powered mining shovels, the 2-cubic-yard 1200WL and 4-cubic-yard 1400WL. These were followed in 1934 with the introduction of the world's first shovel type to be of an all-welded construction, the 3/8-cubic-yard Model 100. Before this, shovels had been a mixture of welded and riveted fabrications. In February 1935, the company shipped its first Model 100. With the introduction of electric-powered and all-welded shovel designs, P&H had positioned itself well for the future of the production of quarry and mining shovels for the rest of the 20th century and beyond.

One of P&H's closest rivals for the type of shovels it built in the mid-20th century was Lima. Originally founded in Lima, Ohio, as Carnes, Harper and Company, it was not until 1877 that the name Lima Machine Works was used for the first time. Early products saw agricultural equipment, sawmills, boilers, steam traction engines, and locomotives, including the famous "Shay" logging engines from 1880. In 1892, the company name changed once again to the Lima Locomotive and Machine Works after the merger of the Lima Machine Works and Lima Car Works. Then in 1916,

Northwest 180-D

Northwest Engineering's largest cable shovel offering was its model 180-D from 1962. Originally designed as a 4.5-cubic-yard-capacity machine, a 180-D Series II was offered in the 1970s equipped with a 6-cubic-yard dipper. Average working weight for the shovel was in the neighborhood of 130 tons. This 180-D is at work in May 1962 loading a 45-ton-capacity Euclid R-45 hauler. *Author's collection*

true "production" excavator-type machine. Not long after the creation of these machines, P&H introduced wheel-type bucket trenchers. The company's first dragline excavator, the 1.25-cubic-yard Model 210 appeared in 1914. In 1918, the company's first gasoline-powered excavator was introduced into the marketplace. In 1924, the company changed its name to the Harnischfeger Corporation, but most in the industry would simply refer to the company by the P&H machine trademark identification. This is true even today.

Bucyrus Erie 120-B

The Bucyrus Erie 120-B is considered the earthmoving industry's first true, heavy-duty, full-revolving, two-crawler mining shovel. Released in 1925, the 120-B was equipped with a 4-cubic-yard dipper and was meant as a replacement for railroad-type loading shovels in the mining industry. Though primarily an electric-powered shovel, some of the earliest units were specified with steam power. This 172-ton electric 120-B is at work in a quarry loading a 30-ton-capacity Euclid in 1963. *Author's collection*

the company name was shortened to simply Lima Locomotive Works. It would not be until 1928 that excavators were finally added to the company roster after it purchased the Ohio Power Shovel Company. Its first gasoline shovel design, the 1.25-cubic-yard Lima 101, was actually just a redesignated Ohio Power Shovel "Ohio Single-Line Gasoline Shovel." The Ohio Power Shovel Company remained a subsidiary of Lima Locomotive until 1934, when it was merged into the parent company as its Shovel and Crane Division.

As the years went by for Lima, its name and company structure would go through still more changes. In 1947, Lima Locomotive merged with the General Machinery Corporation, forming the Lima-Hamilton Corporation. Then, in 1950, it

became part of Baldwin Locomotive Works, forming the new firm of the Baldwin-Lima-Hamilton Corporation, better known as B-L-H. In 1951, B-L-H added the well-respected manufacturer earthmoving machinery Austin-Western to its company's holdings. This gave the company a full line of heavy equipment that would meet the needs of all but the largest quarry and mining operations. Finally, in 1971, Clark Equipment purchased the Lima and Austin-Western product lines from B-L-H. From this point on, the company's excavators were sold under the name Clark-Lima or simply as Clark, until excavator production ceased in 1981.

During its shovel manufacturing years, Lima produced quite a few machine model types that

Bucyrus Erie 190-B

For an 8-cubic-yard mining shovel in the 1950s, they didn't come any better than the Bucyrus Erie 190-B. Originally introduced in 1952, the electric-powered 190-B was an extremely popular shovel for the company. Weighing approximately 275 tons, it could be found operating in quarries and mines the world over. In 1968 it was replaced by the 12-cubic-yard 195-B. Shown here at work in February 1963 is a 190-B loading a 62-ton-capacity Euclid R-62. *Author's collection*

Bucyrus Erie 71-B

Bucyrus Erie introduced its popular 71-B series in 1954. Rated as a 3-cubic-yard excavator, the 71-B could be ordered configured as a shovel, a backhoe, a dragline, a clamshell, or as a lifting crane. Power was supplied by a single Detroit Diesel 6-110 engine rated at 230 flywheel horsepower. Average weight for the shovel model was 94 tons. Other models of the excavator included the 71-B Series II and Series III machines. *Author's collection*

Bucyrus Erie 88-B

Of all the diesel-powered shovels built by Bucyrus Erie, it is its 88-B series, originally introduced in 1946, that stands out as one of the great cable excavator designs of its time. Originally rated as a 4-cubic-yard machine, it would increase to 5 cubic yards with the introduction of the Series II in 1960. Other models to follow were the Series III in 1962 and the 5.5-cubic-yard Series IV in 1968. This 88-B is shown at work in 1963 loading a 45-ton-capacity Euclid R-45 hauler. Average working weight of an early shovel model was approximately 127 tons. *Author's collection*

were in the small- to medium-size ranges, perfect for general contracting work. For shovels with capacities of 3 cubic yards or larger, the company offered eight models. These included the model 1201 in 1940, the 2000 in 1946, the 1601 in 1955, the 1250 in 1957, the 1800 in 1959, the 1850 in 1962, the 1200 in 1963, and the 2400 in 1948. All of these models were well suited to large earthmoving jobs of the day, including quarry work. The size of the 2400 especially allowed it to compete not only in large quarry operations, but surface mining as well. The first series of 2400 Lima shovels was built from 1948 to 1967. These were rated as 6-cubic-yard machines and weighed 18 tons. In 1967, the 2400B was introduced carrying an 8-cubic-yard dipper and a working weight of 237 tons. It ended production in 1981. In 1979, a special edition Clark 2400B-LS model was unveiled. By the time this model was

introduced, Lima excavators were simply referred to as Clarks. The 2400B-LS carried a 12.75-cubic-yard bucket, the largest ever for a standard Lima/Clark cable shovel. Its working weight of 254 tons also put it at the top of its class. But as impressive as the 2400B-LS looked on paper, it was already outdated by the time the first unit went to work. Hydraulic excavators were now king in the earthmoving industry in size classes like the 2400B-LS. Even rubber-tired wheel loaders were of sizes that competed directly with the big shovel. The economic recession of the early 1980s was the straw that finally broke the camel's back when it came to the 2400 series. In 1981, production came to an end for the 2400B and 2400B-LS. In all, 362 units were built of the original 2400 and 294 of the 2400B (both shovel and dragline variations), with only two 2400B-LS shovels produced.

Bucyrus Erie 88-B

The Bucyrus Erie 88-B was considered the "Cadillac" of the industry for a 5-cubic-yard shovel. This 135-ton 88-B Series III, at work in 1964, featured a single Cummins diesel engine, torque converter drive, full air-operating controls, and twin governor-dual controls, which allowed the operator to match the engine and torque converter outputs to meet specific job requirements. Along with the shovel version, the 88-B could also be ordered configured as a dragline, a clamshell, or a lifting crane. *Author's collection*

Above: **Marion 4161**

The Marion 4161 was one of the company's more popular mining shovels during the late 1930s and 1940s. Released in 1935, the 4161 was rated as a 6-cubic-yard shovel, and weighed 215 tons in shovel form. A 199-ton dragline version was also available. Primarily an electric excavator, two specially built steam-powered units were shipped to Russia in 1940. *Author's collection*

Right: **Marion 191-M**

Marion built its first 191-M series mining shovel in 1951, and for a time it was the world's largest two-crawler shovel. The original 191-M was equipped with a standard 10-cubic-yard dipper, but later versions would get 11-cubic-yard units. Operating weight was 386 tons in diesel-powered form or 355 tons when configured as an electric shovel. Pictured in 1951 is the first 191-M built (a three-diesel-engined version) for Western Contracting Corporation of Sioux City, Iowa, for use at its Wichita Air Force Base project near Moline, Kansas. *Author's collection*

Marion 291-M

When Marion introduced its 291-M in 1962, it claimed the title of the world's largest two-crawler shovel. The 291-M weighed 1,055 tons and was originally equipped with a 15-cubic-yard dipper on a 90-foot boom. Marion built two of these shovels, and both went to Peabody Coal. In the mid-1980s they were shipped out to Peabody's Powder River Coal Company's Rochelle Mine, located south of Gillette, Wyoming, and retrofitted with larger coal-loading dippers. Pictured in October 1995 is one of the 291-Ms, shovel number 101, loading coal haulers with its 36-cubic-yard dipper. Shovel number 102 was equipped with a larger 40-cubic-yard coal bucket. *ECO*

Above: **Marion 204-M "SuperFront"**
The Marion 204-M "SuperFront" shovel was one of the company's most daring excavator designs in its history. Introduced in 1976, it featured a unique front-end design that allowed for a larger dipper size, at the same time lowering the shovel's overall working weight. The variable-pitch dipper also allowed for better control of the bucket while digging. *Author's collection*

Marion 204-M "SuperFront"
The first Marion 204-M "SuperFront" shovels were rated at 26 cubic yards, but later machines, such as this 775-ton 204-M from 1979, carried a 30-cubic-yard dipper. Owned by Energy Fuels Mine of Energy, Colorado, it was one of only two 204-M shovels ever to see work in the United States. Oddly enough, in 1989 it was sold to Ulan Coal Mines, Ltd., and shipped to its coal-mining operations in New South Wales, Australia. *Author's collection*

P&H 1055

Introduced around 1950, the P&H 1055 model line was the largest diesel-powered cable shovel produced by the company. With a standard bucket capacity of 4 cubic yards and an average working weight of 103 tons, it was an ideal medium-sized large-construction or quarry shovel. *Author's collection*

Below: **P&H 1055B**

The P&H 1055 featured the company's unique "Magnetorque" electric swing motors that eliminated all friction on swing and propel motions of the excavator. In 1950, P&H also introduced an all-electric-powered 1055E variation. Pictured at work in the early 1960s is a P&H 1055B loading a truck with its 4-cubic-yard dipper. *Author's collection*

Northwest Engineering of Green Bay, Wisconsin, was another excavator manufacturer that had a long history of building very reliable and productive cable shovels for construction and quarry duties. Its heritage can be tracked back to 1910, when a firm by the name of the Hartman-Greiling Company was founded. Primarily a supplier of boilers and machine shop services, the company at this time did not build excavators. By 1918, the company's name had changed to Northwest Engineering Works. In 1920, the company built its first prototype excavator that would pave the way for a full-production machine in 1921, the 104. Though only of 1.25-cubic-yard capacity, the 104 marked the start of the company's development as primarily a builder of cable shovels, backhoes, draglines, and cranes. It was at this time that the name of the firm changed to the Northwest Engineering Company.

Over the years, the company designed and built quite a few popular excavators for the earth-moving marketplace, including the Model 6 and Model 8 of the early 1930s. In 1933, the company introduced its very popular 80 series, which would become the 80-D in 1937. The 80-D series of cable shovels and draglines was a solid sales success with the company. In shovel form, the 80-D started out as a 2.5-cubic-yard machine, but was eventually upgraded to 3 cubic yards. The size of the unit made it the perfect choice for large contractors as well as smaller quarry operators. By the time the unit was discontinued in the early 1980s, more than 2,600 had been put into service worldwide. For customers wanting something a little bit bigger shovel-wise, Northwest offered the

P&H 1600

In 1944, P&H introduced its very popular 1400 series of mining shovels, followed up by the equally successful model 1600 in 1946. The 4.5-cubic-yard 1400 and 6-cubic-yard 1600 established P&H as a true competitor to the likes of Bucyrus Erie and Marion in the production of modern, heavy-duty, electric mining shovels. Shown at work in June 1961 is a freshly painted early version of a P&H 1600, loading a 27-ton-capacity Euclid R-27 hauler. *Author's collection*

Below: **P&H 2800XPA LR**

In June 1988, P&H placed its first 2800XPA shovel into service at Powder River Coal Company's Rochelle Mine, located in the Powder River Basin of Wyoming. The first 2800XPA was specified with a 43-cubic-yard dipper (later reduced to 40 cubic yards) on a 58-foot boom. In late 1997, the mine had P&H modify the XPA into a long-range coal-loading shovel. Today, the 2800XPA LR is equipped with a 64-cubic-yard coal dipper on an 80-foot boom. It is shown at work here in October 1998. *ECO*

180-D. Released in 1962, the 180-D cable shovel, and its backhoe model counterpart, the 190-D, were industry favorites for big quarry rock operations, as well as large construction jobs. Originally rated as a 4.5-cubic-yard shovel, the 180-D would eventually be released in an upgraded Series II version in the 1970s that would raise the standard capacity to 5 cubic yards and 6 for the heavy-duty configuration. The 180-D was a true classic. Like its smaller brother, the 80-D, the 180-D would find worldwide industry acceptance. The 180-D wound up as the largest cable shovel ever to be commercially offered by the company. Though it was listed in their 1985 sales catalog as being available, none were built. By 1987, it had been withdrawn entirely. By this time, hydraulic excavators had complete dominion over shovels in the 180-D capacity class.

In 1925, Bucyrus introduced what has been referred to as the industry's first true heavy-duty mining loading shovel, the 120-B. The 120-B was designed especially to survive the daily working rigors often associated with quarry and surface mining operations. It had the heavy-duty build of a railroad-type shovel, plus the full-revolving undercarriage of a stripping shovel. Originally equipped with a 4-cubic-yard dipper, later models would see this increased to 5 cubic yards. Most of the 120-B shovels to see service were specified with electric power, but a small amount were offered with steam power for operations not willing or financially able to part with the past.

P&H 2800XPA LR Dipper

The 64-cubic-yard dipper on the North Antelope Rochelle Complex's (formerly the Rochelle Mine) P&H 2800XPA LR coal-loading shovel is the second largest in use at the mine site. The largest is the 80-cubic-yard bucket on the P&H 4100A LR shovel. But even at "only" 64 cubic yards, the dipper on the 2800XPA LR is enormous by anyone's standards. *ECO*

Left: P&H 2800XPB

P&H upgraded its very popular 2800XPA mining shovel in late 1992 with the release of an "XPB" version. The 2800XPB carries a nominal dipper capacity of 46 cubic yards on a 58-foot boom. Average operating weight for the shovel model is 1,121 tons. This 2800XPB working at Barrick Goldstrike near Elko, Nevada, in October 1998, is loading 200-ton-capacity haulers with a heavy-duty 46-cubic-yard dipper. It has been in operation since early 1993. *ECO*

P&H 5700LR "Big Don"

P&H introduced its largest shovel series ever in 1978 in the form of the giant 5700LR. The 5700LR was configured as a long-range shovel, equipped with a 25-cubic-yard bucket on a 90-foot boom, and weighed 1,775 tons. Built for Arch Mineral Corporation's Captain Mine, located near Percy, Illinois, it was officially dedicated into service on May 24, 1978. It was nicknamed "Big Don" after the mine's reclamation director, Don McCaw, in recognition of his many years of service at the mine. *P&H Mining*

P&H 5700LR

The first P&H 5700LR worked continuously at the Captain Mine until it was moved in December 1991 to Arch of West Virginia's Ruffner Mine. It then was converted from a long-range shovel into a more conventional loading shovel, with a shorter boom and 44-cubic-yard dipper. The 5700LR is shown at work here at the Captain Mine in October 1991. *Arch Coal*

The 120-B was in production until 1951, with more than 400 of the shovels put into service worldwide. So rugged and reliable was the design that many were still in use in the 1970s.

Bucyrus (Bucyrus Erie after 1927) went on to release a large number of mining shovel model types over the decades with capacities of 3 cubic yards and up. Some of these included the 3-yard 100-B in 1926, the 5-yard 110-B in 1950, the 6-yard 150-B in 1951, the 12-yard 155-B in 1975, and the 6.5-yard 170-B in 1929. Further models included the 8-yard 190-B in 1952, the 12-yard 195-B in 1968, the 8-yard 270-B in 1960, the 15-yard 280-B in 1962, the 20-yard 290-B in 1979, and the 27-yard 295-B in 1972. During this time period, the 295-B was one of the most popular mining shovels in the world, with capacities ranging from 22 to 45 cubic yards, depending on material being mined. Other versions to follow were the 295BI in 1980, the BII in 1981, and the BIII in 1993.

As Bucyrus Erie's electric mining shovels grew in capacity to keep pace with the demands of the industry, the company introduced new diesel model lines to fill in the gaps with respect to

capacity, for shovels to meet the needs of the expanding construction marketplace. Offerings in the 3-cubic-yard-plus categories included the 3-yard 61-B in 1963, the 3-yard 71-B in 1954, the 4.5-yard 84-B in 1964, and the legendary 4-yard 88-B of 1946. The 88-B was in direct competition with Northwest Engineering's 180-D, and to a lesser extent with the Lima 2400 as well. Though the Lima was larger than the 88-B, mining operations considering the 2400 also would have looked at the 88-B. The 88-B underwent numerous upgrades, which included the 5-yard Series II in 1960, the 5-yard Series III in 1962, and the 5.5-yard Series IV in 1968. Though a 6.75-cubic-yard shovel version was listed for release in the early 1980s, none were reported to have been built. By the time the last unit shipped in 1984, approximately 617 units of the 88-B had been built in all series types, including shovel and dragline configurations. The 88-B is considered by many Bucyrus Erie enthusiasts as the finest all-around diesel shovel design the company ever produced.

The 1920s through the 1970s also saw Marion Power Shovel designing and building truly outstanding

P&H 5700XPA

When it comes to loading shovels, they don't get any bigger than P&H's massive 5700XPA. Weighing a stout 2,100 tons, it is the world's largest two-crawler mining shovel. Bucket capacity is 57.5-cubic-yards with a boom length of 70 feet. Standing tall is Coal and Allied Industries' 5700XPA at its Hunter Valley mining operations located in New South Wales, Australia. The second 5700XPA built, it started operations in July 1991. Only two 5700XPA shovels were produced by P&H. *P&H Mining*

heavy-duty quarry and mining shovels. In 1922, the company introduced its first intermediate-sized mining shovel, the 1.75-cubic-yard Model 37. Crawler mounted with a full-revolving under-carriage, the Model 37 was initially available with steam power, but a redesign of the shovel into a fully electric-powered machine made it a popular choice for the mining industry. More than 330 were built by the end of production in 1929. The Model 37 was just a hint at things yet to come.

Bucyrus had gotten a jump on Marion in the production of large heavy-duty mining shovels with its release of the 4-yard 120-B in 1925. It was not until 1927 that Marion could match the Bucyrus shovel with a machine of its own, the Model 4160. Before the 4160, the largest loading shovel offered by Marion was its 2.25-cubic-yard Type 490 from 1926. The 4160, with its 4-cubic-yard bucket capacity, was as modern as anything

offered by Bucyrus Erie at the time and was considered one of the largest intermediate-sized shovels available to the mining industry during the early 1930s. It would eventually be replaced by the immensely popular 4161 series in 1935. A 6-cubic-yard shovel designed for large quarry and mining operations, the 4161 was a star performer in copper mining operations in the southwestern part of the United States, as well as other hard-rock and ore-digging applications around the world. Though primarily designed as an electric-powered shovel, two were custom built with steam power in 1940 for mining duties in Russia during World War II. In all, 206 units were built of the 4161 series.

Marion, like Bucyrus Erie, produced many popular shovel designs that were 3-plus cubic yards in size. Some of the more notable of these included the 3-cubic-yard 4121 in 1934, the 4.75-yard

Right: **Bucyrus Erie 395-B**

The Bucyrus Erie 395-B shovel series has enjoyed a long life in the company's product line since it was first released in 1980. This 36-cubic-yard 395-B shovel photographed in 2001 is working at Syncrude's Base Mine loading a 240-ton-capacity Caterpillar 793B hauler. Originally part of a group of four 395-B shovels delivered to Syncrude starting in late 1985, it is one of three still remaining on active duty today. *Keith Haddock*

Below: **Marion 301-M**

In July 1986, Marion placed its first 301-M electric mining shovel into operation at the Mt. Newman Mine, located in the Pilbara iron ore range of Western Australia. It was equipped with an extra-heavy-duty 36-cubic-yard dipper, rated at 70 tons, specially suited to the high-density material it would be working in, and a 53-foot, 6-inch boom. Pictured is the prototype 301-M in its first month of service in Australia. *Author's collection*

Marion 301-M

The first Marion 301-M shovel to be sold in the United States went to the AMAX Belle Ayr Mine in Wyoming. Dedicated into service in March 1991, it was equipped with a 54-cubic-yard bucket, rated at 85 tons capacity. It carried a 60-foot boom, weighed 1,150 tons, and could load the mine's 240-ton-capacity Unit Rig Lectra Haul MT-4000 haulers in three passes of its dipper. It is shown here in October 1995. *ECO*

4162 in 1937, the 3-yard 101-M in 1953, and the 4.5-yard 111-M in 1946. Other models were the 6-yard 151-M in 1945, the 9-yard 181-M in 1956, the 10-yard 182-M in 1966, the 8-yard 183-M in 1956, and the record-breaking 11-yard 191-M in 1951. The 191-M in particular was a real standout in the Marion product line. In its day, it was the largest mining shovel available on two crawlers. Though most were electric powered, five of the units were built with diesel power. Produced until 1989, the 191-M was a solid sales success with 157 units shipped.

Another shovel introduction by Marion in 1962 would again set a world record for the largest mining shovel on two crawlers. Identified as the 291-M, the model weighed a record 1,055 tons. The original 291-M shovels were configured with long-range 90-foot booms and 15-cubic-yard dippers. Though the model was offered with a 65-foot, 25-yard setup, none were produced. Only two 291-M shovels were eventually built, both for Peabody Coal. One was shipped in 1962 to Peabody's Sinclair Mine in Kentucky, while the other went to its Lynnville Mine in Indiana in 1963. After many

Marion 301-M

The Marion 301-M shovels were some of the finest excavators ever built by Marion. Of the 14 produced, all were still in full active duty around the world at the time of this writing. Of the three 301-M shovels in the United States, all are operated by RAG Coal West: two at its Eagle Butte Mine and one at its Belle Ayr operation, which is the one shown here. *ECO*

years working at these operations, both units were shipped out to the Powder River Basin in Wyoming for duties at Powder River Coal's Rochelle Mine, a subsidiary of Peabody. Both shovels were retrofitted with larger 36- and 40-cubic-yard dippers for coal-loading operations.

In 1975, Marion introduced its 201-M series mining shovel. With a nominal bucket capacity of 24 cubic yards and a working range of 18 to 40 cubic yards, the 201-M was in direct competition with the Bucyrus Erie 295-B. Both machines were comparable in size, with the Marion tipping the scales at 676 tons and the Bucyrus Erie weighing 670 tons. Later versions of both shovels increased in weight considerably. Marion delivered its last 201-M into service in early 1990.

The 1970s also saw Marion introduce a revolutionary shovel design, the 204-M "SuperFront." SuperFront referred to its radical front-end design. The unique front-end geometry of the design allowed the shovel to have increased dipper capacity, a lower overall working weight, and a better center of gravity. The design also featured a variable-pitch dipper that allowed better bucket control while digging. Nominal bucket capacity was rated at 30 cubic yards, with a bucket selection range of 20 to 45 yards. Operating weight was right at 775 tons in full operating trim.

The development of the SuperFront actually dated back to 1967, when Marion engineers retrofitted a standard 101-M shovel with a prototype front-end assembly equipped with a 5-cubic-yard dipper. Results from this test machine were used on a larger prototype shovel design called the 194-M. In 1972, the company fabricated its first 194-M out of an original 191-M model located at the Reserve Mining Company in Minnesota. This unit utilized a 16-cubic-yard bucket. A second 191-M was also modified into a second 194-M at the Cyprus-Pima Mining Company in Arizona. This shovel had a 21-cubic-yard dipper. After extensive testing of both units, a production model of the SuperFront was officially announced in 1974 as the 204-M. The first 204-M SuperFront shovels were built for use in a Russian mining operation in 1976 and were fabricated under license by Sumitomo Heavy Industries of Japan. Unique to these units were their hydraulic-crowd designs and 26-cubic-yard bucket capacities. Later models

Marion 301-M

The third Marion 301-M shovel to be sold in the United States went to Cyprus Mountain Coal Corporation's Starfire Mine in Bulan, Kentucky, in late 1993. Equipped with a 56-cubic-yard dipper with an 85-ton load rating, it was capable of loading the mine's 170-ton haulers in two passes and the 240-tonners in three. It is shown at work in August 1995. *ECO*

Marion 301-M

In 1996, Cyprus Mountain Coal's Starfire Marion 301-M was shipped out to the Cyprus AMAX Belle Ayr Mine, located just south of Gillette, Wyoming. There, it was converted from a single-cab shovel to a dual-cab version, the only 301-M to be so configured. This is the converted 301-M at the Belle Ayr Mine, operating in October 1998. In early 2001, the new owners of the mine, RAG Coal West, had the big Marion moved to its Eagle Butte Mine, just north of Gillette. *ECO*

of the 204-M were equipped with a cable-crowd design and 30-cubic-yard dippers. Over the next five years, the Russians eventually purchased 10 SuperFront shovels. The first North American deliveries of the 204-M were in 1979.

The SuperFront shovel design was a daring engineering exercise for Marion, to say the least. But the complicated design of the shovel meant there was a greater possibility of things going wrong. Even though the shovel did have a few bugs in it, it performed remarkably well in the field. But as far as the mining industry was concerned, there simply was too much innovation in the 204-M for its own good. In all, 17 units were built of the 204-M, with the last four 34-cubic-yard shovels shipping to Ok Tedi Mining Limited's copper mine in Papua, New Guinea, between 1987 and 1988.

As with Bucyrus Erie and Marion, P&H offered a broad array of diesel, electric, and diesel-electric mining shovel designs with capacities of 2.5 cubic yards and larger. Some of the company's earliest offerings in these size classes were the 3-cubic-yard Model 850 and 860 and the 3.5-yard Model 870, all in 1929. Others included the 3.5-yard Model 900 and 900A in 1928, the 2.5-yard 955 (early version) in 1940, the 3-yard 1025 in 1958, the 3.5-yard 1025A in 1960, the 3-yard 1055 (early version) in 1938, and the 3.5-yard 1055E (electric) in 1950. Shovel models designed around the use of Ward-Leonard electric controls, in addition to the ones mentioned earlier, include the 2.25-yard 1225WL in 1936, the 2.5-yard 1250WL in 1937, the 3-yard 1300WL in 1935, and the 5-yard 1500WL in 1942.

P&H's more modern range of electric mining shovels as we know them today share their origins with the 4.5-yard 1400 of 1944 and the 6-yard 1600 of 1946. The look and performance of these machines would be the pattern for the company's shovel designs for decades to come. Other popular electric-powered mining shovels included the 5-yard 1500 in 1951, the 8-yard 1800 in 1955, the 11-yard 1900 in 1964, and the 12-yard 2100 in 1963. Even though a 7-yard 1700 series was proposed in 1956 and a 10-yard 2000 in 1961, none were ever built. From the late 1940s through the 1950s, P&H also offered a series of diesel-electric models that did not require the use of an external power source. These included the 4-yard 1300DE, the 4.5-yard 1400DE, and the 4-yard 1500DE.

Bucyrus Erie 495-BI

The first Bucyrus 495-BI was originally equipped with a 60-cubic-yard dipper, rated at 85 tons capacity. After a few months of operation, the bucket was reduced to 56 cubic yards in volume capacity. The 495-BI carries a 64-foot boom length and has an operating weight of 1,228 tons. *ECO*

Marion 351-M

Currently the largest coal-loading shovel in the world is the Marion 351-M LR. Built for Thunder Basin Coal Company's Black Thunder Mine, located near Wright, Wyoming, it is equipped with a huge 84-cubic-yard coal-loading dipper, rated at 64 tons capacity. It carries a 75-foot boom and weighs 1,335 tons in full working trim. It is also the only 351-M shovel to be equipped with dual operator's cabs. It was dedicated into service at the mine in June 1996. *ECO*

Opposite: **Marion 351-M**

The third and last Marion-built 351-M mining shovel to be placed in service was for Fording River Coal, located near Elkford, British Columbia, Canada. Officially commissioned on July 29, 1996, the 351-M HR carries a 56-cubic-yard, 85-ton-capacity dipper on a 60-foot boom. Working weight was listed at 1,253 tons. It is shown here loading a 240-ton-capacity Dresser 830E Haulpak in 1996. *Bucyrus International*

Of all of P&H's early electric mining shovel offerings, none was as dramatic as its 2800 series. Introduced into service in 1969, the 2800, with its 25-cubic-yard bucket capacity, was the world's largest-*capacity* mining loading shovel on two crawlers. The key word here is *capacity*. With an operating weight of 906 tons, the first 2800 shovels were not as large as the two 1,055-ton Marion 291-Ms produced, but they did carry a larger standard rock bucket. The P&H 2800 series mining shovels were also the first designed by the company to use its Electrotorque system for converting AC electrical input into DC operating power. The first four 2800 shovels to be built were all for Kaiser Resources for use at its Balmer Mine site in British Columbia, Canada. Even today, one of these original 2800 shovels is listed as being on active duty at the mine, which is now owned by Teck Corporation and renamed the Elkview Mine.

Not long after the introduction of the original 2800 series, P&H launched a slightly smaller mining shovel in the form of the 2300. Released in 1972, the 2300 was classified as a 22-cubic-yard shovel, with an operating weight of 650 tons. Other variations of the series included the 27-yard 2300XP in 1981, the 28-yard 2300XPA in 1989, and the 33-yard 2300XPB in 1994, which is still current at the time of this writing.

As the 2300 series grew in size, so did the 2800 model line. In 1982, the 30-yard 2800XP was introduced, followed by the 36-yard 2800XPA in 1988. Then in 1992, the largest of the series, the 46-yard 2800XPB, was put into service. Weighing 1,121 tons in standard form, it is the heaviest of all the 2800 series machines and is still in production today.

As the 1970s drew to a close, P&H had one more trick up its sleeve: the 5700 series mining shovel. Simply put, the P&H 5700 machines were the world's largest two-crawler mining shovels, dwarfing even the Marion 291-M series. Originally introduced in 1978, the first shovel built, a long-range 5700LR, was equipped with a 25-cubic-yard dipper on a 90-foot boom. But what made the 5700LR so spectacular was its bulk, which topped out at 1,775 tons in full operating trim. The 5700LR was built for operations at Arch of Illinois'

Above: Bucyrus 595-B

After Bucyrus International acquired Marion Power Shovel in 1997, it continued to market the 351-M as the Bucyrus 351M-ST. In 1999 the company officially changed the shovel's nomenclature to 595-B. As of 2003, all of the 57-cubic-yard, 1,300-ton 595-B shovels are operated by Suncor Energy, located north of Fort McMurray, Alberta, Canada. *ECO*

Right: P&H 4100

In 1991, P&H introduced its 4100 series electric mining shovel. Designed for three-pass loading of 240-ton haul trucks, the 4100 was an immediate success for the company. Nominal dipper capacity of the early 4100 shovels was 56 cubic yards, with an 85-ton payload limit and a 60-foot boom. Working weight of the shovel was 1,175 tons. This 4100 is working in October 1995 at Powder River Coal's Caballo Mine located just south of Gillette, Wyoming, which is also the home of the first 4100 to be delivered into service. *ECO*

Captain Mine, which also was the home of the world's largest shovel of any type, the Marion 6360. Nicknamed "Big Don," the first 5700LR was originally painted green. But in the late 1980s, the shovel was repainted white, blue, and red. In December 1991, the shovel was moved to Arch of West Virginia's Ruffner Mine, where it was updated with a shorter boom and a 44-cubic-yard bucket. In 1999, it was also retrofitted with P&H's latest digital drive technology, greatly improving the shovel's cycle times, as well as increasing the machine's overall productivity.

Four more 5700 models were eventually built by P&H. The second unit produced, a 60-cubic-yard 5700, was shipped in 1981 to Bloomfield Collieries' Hunter Valley mine site in Australia. The third unit was actually a barge-mounted version of the 5700, custom built for Great Lakes Dredge

Right: **P&H 4100A**
This P&H 4100A is making its way to a new digging site within the North Antelope Rochelle Complex (NARC) in the Powder River Basin. The shovel carries its electric trailing line with its bucket as it makes its way down to a lower bench. Identified as shovel 107, this 4100A was delivered to NARC in late 1996 and is equipped with a 56-cubic-yard dipper. *ECO*

Left: **P&H 4100A**
P&H released an updated "A" version of its popular mining shovel in 1994. The 4100A featured a slightly longer 64-foot boom, a strengthened dipper handle, along with a host of other electrical and mechanical improvements. Though the nominal dipper capacity was the same as the previous model, operating weight was now up to 1,336 tons. At work at P&M's Kemmerer Mine in western Wyoming in May 2002 is their 56-cubic-yard 4100A. This shovel was delivered new in 1996. *ECO*

and Dock Company in 1987. Christened the
"Chicago," it could be configured as a 28-cubic-
yard shovel dredge or a 50-yard clamshell dredge.
Shovels four and five were 5700XPA machines,
both equipped with 57.5-cubic-yard dippers and
destined for Australia. Weighing an incredible
2,100 tons each, they are the largest two-crawler
mining shovels ever produced. Shovel four was
shipped to R. W. Miller and Company's Mount
Thorley Mine, located near Newcastle, New South
Wales, in late 1990. The fifth unit was shipped in
1991 to Coal and Allied Industries' Hunter Valley
mining operations, also located in New South
Wales. Today, all of the 5700/5700XPA mining
shovels are on the active duty lists, but the same

cannot be said for the dredge hybrid unit. On
October 5, 1996, while the barge was en route to a
new working location off the coast of Denmark,
the "Chicago" was swamped by high waves 60
miles from the Esbjerg port. The waves capsized
the barge and sent it to the bottom of the North
Sea. It was deemed too expensive to salvage.

The P&H 5700 series of mining shovels was
not the success the company had hoped for. The
shovel was designed to load a new generation of
ultra-large-capacity haulers, such as the 350-
ton-capacity Terex 33-19 Titan, but the worldwide economic recession of the early 1980s
killed the market for such a large truck. Without
a suitably sized hauler to be paired with, the

5700 was simply out of step with the changing times. By the time the economics improved in the mining industry, shovel designs that were lighter and faster cycling, but of similar capacities to the 5700, were now being offered, including new designs by P&H itself.

For the most part, the big three of Bucyrus Erie, Marion, and P&H have had the large cable mining shovel marketplace to themselves for the last 25 years or so. Though both Russia and China produced cable mining shovels of their own designs, they were primarily built for their respective home markets and were simply not in the same league as the state-of-the-art designs coming out of North America.

One of the top mining shovel models of the 1980s was the Bucyrus Erie 395-B series. Originally announced in 1979, the first unit was not placed into service until 1980. Nominal bucket capacity for the 395-B was 34 cubic yards, with a bucket range of 25 to 60 yards. The shovel design was also Bucyrus Erie's first to feature its new ACUTROL AC electric motors, instead of the more usual static DC type. With a working weight of 916 tons, it was in direct competition with P&H's 2800 series mining shovel. The prototype 395-B would make its first home at Anamax Mining Company's Twin Buttes Mine, near Tucson, Arizona. Other variations to follow in the footsteps of the original model included the 395-BII in 1989 and the 395-

P&H 4100A

The ASARCO Mission Mine placed its second 4100A shovel (unit 519) into service just a few weeks after its first 4100A, shovel 518, was dedicated in July 1996. Equipped with the same 60-cubic-yard dipper as the first 4100A, the second shovel takes a big 85-ton bite of earth at the Mission Mine in October 1998. *ECO*

P&H 4100A

Working up against the mining face, nothing can beat the productivity of a large cable mining shovel for high-volume earthmoving work. This P&H 4100A operating at Powder River Coal's Caballo Mine in June 2000, demonstrates the awesome digging might of its large 59-cubic-yard dipper. *ECO*

P&H 4100A

The P&H 4100A featured an offset cab that allowed the operator a clear field of sight for all of the shovel's digging and dumping functions. A good operator at the controls could average 30 seconds or less per loading cycle. *ECO*

BIII in 1995, which is still presently offered in the company's product line as of 2003.

Not to be outgunned by either Bucyrus Erie or P&H in the 1980s, Marion introduced a heavy hitter of its own that would give the Bucyrus Erie 395-B and P&H 2800XP something a bit more substantial to contend with. That new shovel design was the Marion 301-M. Launched into service in 1986, the 301-M was a true heavy-weight in the mining shovel marketplace. Due to the financial straits of the company in the early 1980s, Marion was not able to counter the top shovel offerings of its rivals. But with the intro-duction of the 301-M, the company had a shovel model that could go toe-to-toe with the likes of a 2800XP or 395-B. The first 301-M shovels weighed approximately 1,047 tons, with later versions weighing 1,150 tons. The big Marion carried a nominal dipper capacity of 54 cubic yards, with an 80-ton payload capacity. The prototype machine, shipped to the Mt. Newman Mine in Western Australia's Pilbara iron ore range, was equipped with a smaller 36-yard, 70-ton-capacity bucket. This was to offset the extremely heavy and abrasive iron ore material

the shovel was digging in. In all, 14 units of the 301-M were put into service worldwide, includ-ing 4 in Australia, 2 in Siberia, 5 in Canada, and 3 in the United States.

To counter the Marion 301-M threat, Bucyrus Erie introduced a slightly larger offering in 1990 called the 495-B. With a nominal dipper capacity of 55 cubic yards, an 85-ton payload capacity, and a working weight of 1,228 tons, the 495-B was more than 114 tons heavier than the company's own 395-BII shovel design then available. In 1996, the company released an updated 495-BI version of the shovel with a host of performance and control upgrades. Even though it was a new model, working bucket capacities, as well as weight, were not changed.

The fortunes and well-being of the big three cable mining manufacturers was a roller coaster ride for much of the 1990s. Early in that decade, Bucyrus Erie was on shaky financial ground and P&H looked like it could do no wrong. By the end of the decade, Bucyrus was looking lean and mean, and now it was P&H's turn to feel the wrath of the shareholders and accountants alike. Marion just squeaked by through most of it.

P&H 4100A

When a shovel is shut down by failure or for a scheduled preventive maintenance service, better known as a PM, service trucks from all points within the mine descend upon the shovel to take care of any repairs required as quickly and safely as possible. This 56-cubic-yard P&H 4100A operating at Fording River Coal, located in British Columbia, Canada, in October 1997, is in the process of undergoing a scheduled PM service. *ECO*

P&H 4100A LR

In September 1995, P&H placed a very special, one-of-a-kind shovel into service called the 4100A LR. Built for Powder River Coal's North Antelope Mine (now North Antelope Rochelle Complex), it is equipped with a massive 80-cubic-yard coal-loading dipper on an 80-foot boom. Overall working weight of the long-range coal-loading shovel is 1,349 tons. It is shown here in June 2000 loading a Caterpillar 797 hauler, which is capable of carrying approximately 386 tons of coal in its special, large-volume coal body. *ECO*

As Bucyrus Erie's North American sales declined during the 1990s, its share of the overseas marketplace increased. To better reflect the times, the company felt a name change was in order. In early 1996, the company renamed itself Bucyrus International to better reflect its position in the global mining sales marketplace. But the really big move for the company would transpire in April 1997, when Bucyrus International signed a letter of intent to purchase the Marion Power Shovel Company. And just like that, on August 16, Marion's 113 years of producing some of the world's finest excavators came to an end. They had been rivals for over a century, but now it was over. Bucyrus now owned it all. Key design and engineering personnel were transferred up to South Milwaukee from Marion, Ohio. Once the old manufacturing plant had been cleaned out, the Marion facilities were put up for sale. The Marion name and trademark were also casualties of the buyout.

Though Marion was now no more, it did go out on a high note, at least as far as its big mining shovel designs were concerned. In 1995, Marion introduced an upgraded version of the 301-M series called the 351-M. Looking much like its predecessor, the 351-M was slightly larger, with a nominal dipper capacity of 56 cubic yards, with an 85-ton payload rating and a working weight of approximately 1,300 tons. Marion was able to build three of these shovels before it was purchased by Bucyrus. The first of these was sold to Suncor for use at its tar sands operations north of Fort McMurray, Alberta, and was identified as a 351-M ST. The second machine was destined for the Black Thunder Mine in the Powder River Basin of Wyoming in 1996. Referred to as the 351-M LR, it carried a long-range 75-foot boom and a massive 84-cubic-yard, 63-ton-capacity coal-loading bucket. It also has the distinction of being the only 351-M to have been factory equipped with dual operating cabs. Working weight was listed at 1,335 tons. Even today, this unit is considered the world's largest coal-loading shovel. The last of the big Marions was shipped to Fording River Coal, located near Elkford, British Columbia, in 1996. It started work in July, a month after the Black Thunder machine was dedicated into service. Identified as the 351-M HR, it carried a 56-cubic-yard dipper. After the buyout by Bucyrus, the shovel model continued to be marketed as the 351M-ST. In 1999, Bucyrus officially changed the nomenclature of the shovel

to the 595-B, to conform with the rest of the company's shovel offerings. As of 2003, all of the Bucyrus 351M-ST/595-B shovels have been built for Suncor Energy for oil sand mining operations.

Though the large shovels of Bucyrus and Marion during the 1990s were truly formidable mining machines, P&H has the distinction of producing what many in the industry consider the finest mining shovel today, the 4100 series. Originally introduced in 1991, the P&H 4100, along with later variations of the model, are the best-selling, ultra-large cable mining shovels in the world today. The original 4100 shovel models' mission in life was clear: to load 240-ton-capacity haul trucks in three quick passes, averaging 30 seconds or less per dipper cycle. The 4100 was capable of swinging a nominal 56-cubic-yard, 85-ton-capacity dipper. Early units of the big P&H shovel tipped the scales at approximately 1,175 tons. As the new shovel matured, its overall working weight steadily increased to about 1,225 tons. The first 4100 built went to work in July 1991 at Carter Mining Company's Caballo Mine, located south of Gillette, Wyoming, and was equipped with a 59-cubic-yard bucket. Today, this

mining operation is owned by the Powder River Coal Company, a subsidiary of Peabody Energy.

As good as the original 4100 shovel design was, there was still room for improvement. This led P&H to introduce an updated version, the 4100A, in 1994. The 4100A introduced many

design improvements, including electrical, mechanical, and structural. Most of the major changes were in the front end, which included a slightly longer boom and a beefed-up dipper handle. Capacity of the "A" model was the same as its predecessor, but operating weight was now up to 1,336 tons.

All P&H 4100A shovels were custom built to match a customer's particular operational needs, such as truck fleet sizes and the weight of the material being mined. This goes for all of the company's shovels being produced today as well. But there was one "A" model that was different from all of the rest. This was the 4100A LR long-range coal-loading shovel built for the North Antelope Mine in the Powder River Basin of Wyoming in 1995. Designed to load coal only, the 1,366-ton 4100A LR is equipped with an 80-foot boom and a massive 80-cubic-yard dipper, the

Above: **P&H 4100XPB**

The first 4100XPB built by P&H is this shovel, which was delivered to Triton's North Rochelle Mine in the Powder River Basin of Wyoming in February 2000. Equipped with a 68-cubic-yard dipper, it can load the mine's 320-ton haulers in just three quick passes. Weight of the shovel is approximately 1,512 tons. It is pictured here loading overburden in June 2000. *ECO*

P&H 4100XPB

Kennecott Energy placed its first P&H 4100XPB into service in May 2001 at its Jacobs Ranch Mine, located near Wright, Wyoming. The 4100XPB is capable of loading the mine's 360-ton-capacity Liebherr T-282 haulers in three quick passes with its 120-ton-payload bucket. It is shown at work here in May 2002. *ECO*

largest ever fabricated by the company in volume size. It is second only to the 84-yard Marion 351-M LR working just a few miles away at another coal mining operation. Though only one was ever built, it has proven to be one of the most productive of all the "A" shovel machines.

In late 1999, P&H shipped its first 4100XPB. The 4100A was a big machine. The 4100XPB was bigger still. Designed as a replacement for the "A" model, the XPB version was built for the new generation of ultra-large mining haulers coming into the marketplace. With a nominal dipper capacity rating of 67 cubic yards and 100-ton payload, the 4100XPB has the ability to load 320-ton haulers in three passes in standard form. A working weight of 1,569-tons also makes it the heaviest of all 4100 series shovels. The 4100XPB also incorporates three swing motors and the company's own highly advanced DC digital drive technology, which allows the shovel to achieve subcycle times of below 29 seconds. Units have actually achieved times of approximately 26 seconds, which is incredible for a shovel the size of the 4100XPB. The shovel was designed using state-of-the-art CAD (computer-aided design) and FEA (finite element analysis) software programs, including the fifth generation of CATIA

Top: **P&H 4100XPB**

This P&H 4100XPB, operating at the Jacobs Ranch Mine, is able to move to various working locations within the mine by simply picking up its specially designed sled-mounted cable reel with its dipper. Notice just how large the shovel's 77-cubic-yard bucket is as it loads a 320-ton-capacity hauler. *ECO*

Above: **P&H 4100XPB Crawler**

As one might expect, it takes a set of very robust crawlers to support the weight of a P&H 4100XPB shovel, which in present form, tips the scales at 1,569 tons in full operating trim. Each of the shovel's crawlers is 38 feet, 6 inches long, with the standard width of the track shoes measuring 76 inches. Each link weighs 2 tons, and there are 42 of them per crawler assembly. *ECO*

P&H 4100XPB

The first Jacobs Ranch' 4100XPB (number 1212) was originally fitted with a 76-cubic-yard dipper, but later a special bucket lip kit was installed that increased capacity by 1 yard. Here, the 4100XPB has a 120-ton payload in its 77-cubic-yard dipper as it awaits a truck to back into position. *ECO*

(computer-aided three-dimensional interactive application). Nothing was left to chance concerning the 4100XPB's design.

The first 4100XPB officially went to work in February 2000 at Triton's North Rochelle Mine in the Powder River Basin. The 4100XPB was an immediate success in the marketplace. Orders started coming in from all of the company's key sales areas, especially North and South America. Three 4100XPB shovels in particular, delivered in 2001 and 2002 to the Powder River Basin, stand out from all the rest. These machines, one operating at RAG Coal's Belle Ayr Mine (delivered 2001) and two at Kennecott's Jacob Ranch Mine (delivered 2001 and 2002), are all equipped with huge 77-cubic-yard dippers, carrying payload ratings of 120 tons each. As far as payload weight is concerned, these are simply the largest capacity buckets the company has ever fabricated. These massive buckets are designed for three-pass loading of 360-ton haul trucks. Even though P&H offered in the past its giant 5700XPA shovel designs with an optional 120-ton dipper, none was ever built. In 2003, RAG Coal's 4100 XPB dipper was replaced with an even larger 82-cubic-yard unit, though the payload capacity remained unchanged at 120 tons.

Another branch of the P&H 4100 series family of specialized offerings are the oil sands mining shovels. The first of these was the 4100TS, which was designed to cope with the specialized digging requirements found in the oil sands mining area located north of Fort McMurray, Alberta. The material being mined is extremely abrasive, so extra-heavy-duty buckets with additional wear guards are needed. The shovels are also equipped with extra-wide crawler pads measuring 138 inches across. The material the shovel has to work on at times has the consistency of something resembling a mattress, so the extra-wide pads are necessary to give the 1,489-ton shovel good floatation and a stable working foundation. The latest P&H DC digital drive system is also incorporated into the design. The first of these special "TS" models was shipped to Suncor Energy in 1998 with a 57-cubic-yard, 100-ton-capacity dipper. In 1999, Syncrude Canada purchased its first 4100TS shovel, equipped with a 58-cubic-yard bucket. Additional units for both companies would follow. In 2001, P&H introduced an upgraded version of

P&H 4100XPB

In June 2002, Kennecott Energy placed its second 1,569-ton P&H 4100XPB shovel into operation at its Jacobs Ranch Mine. The shovel (number 1214) is an exact duplicate of the first 4100XPB the mine placed in operation the year before. It is shown here in September 2002 loading a 360-ton-capacity Liebherr T-282 hauler with its 77-cubic-yard, 120-ton payload dipper. *ECO*

P&H 4100TS

P&H introduced its 4100TS in 1998 to meet the specialized digging demands often required from mining shovels working in the oil sands of northern Alberta. This 4100TS shovel, shown loading a 386-ton-capacity Caterpillar 797 hauler at Syncrude's Base Mine just north of Fort McMurray, Alberta, in October 2001, is equipped with a 58-cubic-yard dipper, rated at 100 tons capacity. It has extra-wide 138-inch crawler pads for better floatation, a 70-foot boom, and weighs 1,489 tons. *ECO*

P&H 4100TS

This P&H 4100TS working at Syncrude's Aurora Mine in 2001 has the exact same specifications as the "TS" shovels working at Syncrude's Base Mine, including the 58-cubic-yard dipper. In all, Syncrude operates four 4100TS shovels: two are at the Aurora Mine, and two are located at the Base Mine. *ECO*

the "TS" shovel called the 4100BOSS. Looking much like the 4100TS, the "BOSS" contains numerous technical upgrades that increased its production advantage over the previous 4100TS model by 28 percent, even though the bucket capacity remains at 58 cubic yards. In 2002, Suncor took delivery of its first 4100BOSS shovel. Also in 2002, P&H won a contract with Syncrude for the delivery of three more BOSS machines. This brings Syncrude's total, as of 2003, to four 4100BOSS and four 4100TS oil sands mining shovels. In total, P&H has sold more than 120 units of all variations of its 4100 series family of highly productive shovels as of 2003.

As productive and popular as the P&H Mining 4100XPB and 4100BOSS shovels are today, there are still alternatives available to the mining industry. Bucyrus International builds three shovels that are in direct response to the top-of-the-line

offerings from its cross-town rival. Its 495-BII and 495HR models are targeted at the same market segment as the 4100XPB. And its latest shovel design, the 495HF, is in direct response to the 4100BOSS shovel.

The Bucyrus 495-BII was originally announced by the company in 2000, with the first machine placed into active service at Peabody Energy's Lee Ranch Mine, located near Grants, New Mexico, in February 2001. Building on the previous success of the 495-BI model, the BII is a far more refined machine with the latest state-of-the-art electronics and computer controls. The BII also has a longer boom, 67 feet versus 64 feet, larger hoist and rope crowd drums, and a beefed-up revolving frame. All of these improvements help raise the BII shovel's standard bucket capacity to 66 cubic yards, with a working selection range of 40 to 80 yards. Payload capacity was

P&H 4100BOSS

In October 2001, P&H commissioned its first 4100BOSS shovel into service at Syncrude's Aurora Mine. The 4100BOSS (B series Oil Sands Shovel) replaces the previous "TS" model type and is 28 percent more productive than its predecessor. This image shows the first "BOSS" shovel on October 15, 2001, going through its final system checks before heading down into the pit for its first taste of oil sand digging. *ECO*

P&H 4100BOSS

It is now October 18, 2001, and Syncrude's P&H 4100BOSS is hard at work at the Aurora Mine. The 4100BOSS dipper size, track width, and boom length is the same as those of the previous 4100TS model, though the new shovel does weigh a bit more at 1,493 tons. It is what you do not see that makes the "BOSS" such a performance standout, such as its advanced digital drive and computer systems. In 2003, Syncrude took delivery of three more "BOSS" shovels. *ECO* originally listed at 100 tons but has since been increased to 110 tons. Working weight is right around 1,344 tons. In 2002, the BII model line was also equipped with the company's new offset "Super-Cab" design, which increases the operator's visibility, as well as comfort and safety, to all-new industry levels.

Bucyrus' next heavy hitter is the 495HF (High-Flotation) shovel, which is a special model designed specifically for digging in oil sands. Dedicated into service in October 2002, the 495HF is the company's first shovel design to use both Bucyrus and Marion technology. The "HF" is essentially the latest 495-BII, equipped with the lower works of its 595-B, which is based on the Marion 351-M series. The shovel is equipped with a 59-cubic-yard, 100-ton-capacity dipper, 140-inch-wide crawler links, and the latest "Super-Cab" design. The shovel's operating weight of 1,450 tons also makes it the heaviest production two-crawler shovel model in the company's history. The first three shovels were purchased by Albian Sands

Bucyrus 495-BII

In February 2001, Bucyrus International placed its first 495-BII mining shovel into service at Peabody Energy's Lee Ranch Mine near Grants, New Mexico. As pictured here in May 2002, its 66-cubic-yard, 110-ton-capacity dipper is loading a 360-ton-capacity Terex MT-5500 hauler. Boom length on the shovel is 67 feet, with an overall working weight of 1,344 tons. In mid-2002, Bucyrus delivered the first 495-BII equipped with its new offset "Super-Cab" design. *ECO*

Energy for use at its new Muskeg River Mine, located north of Fort McMurray, Alberta.

The latest mining shovel introduction by Bucyrus is its 495HR (Hard Rock). The 495HR is essentially the standard shovel configuration of the 495HF. Weighing in at 1,439 tons, with a 110-ton nominal capacity dipper, the shovel features the same under carriage as the oil sands 495HF, but with narrower crawler pads. The first unit shipped in the spring of 2003 to Collahuasi's copper mine in Chile.

Today's modern rope shovels have never been more technologically advanced. Their bucket capacities are approaching sizes once only thought could be handled by the likes of a stripping shovel. But what of the smaller- and intermediate-sized cable machines of yesterday? The answer is simple: they have all been replaced by high-pressure fluid-powered machines. Enter the hydraulic excavator.

Bucyrus 495HF

Bucyrus International's 495HF is the company's answer to P&H's "BOSS" oil sands shovel. The 495HF (High-Flotation) is equipped with a 59-cubic-yard dipper and has a working weight of 1,450 tons. The shovel also features 140-inch-wide track pads and the new, offset "Super-Cab." The first 495HF was dedicated into service on October 1, 2002, at Albian Sands Energy's Muskeg River Mine in Northern Alberta. Pictured in December 2002 is the second 495HF delivered to the mine, at rest between shift changes. *Gary Middlebrook*

Chapter Four

HYDRAULIC MINING EXCAVATORS

For the first half of the 20th century, cable shovels, along with cable backhoes, dominated the construction, quarry, and mining markets. They were the preferred machines for digging and loading in the earthmoving industry. Of course, there really was no alternative choice for the contractor at that time. All of that would change dramatically in the last half of the century with the introduction of the hydraulic excavator. Soon the cable machines would be fighting for their very existence. Life would go on, though a little bumpy, for the larger mining cable shovels. The smaller and midsize cable designs would soon be swept under the waves of obsolescence, however, many becoming mere museum pieces in a relatively short time.

Today's hydraulic excavator can trace its ancestry to just after World War II, when various manufacturers in Italy, France, and the United States started to realize the virtues of the design. Some of the first to crop up after the war were in 1946, when inventor Ray Ferwerda of Cleveland, Ohio, sold the patent rights to a machine he created called the "Gradall" to the Warner and Swasey Company. The design incorporated a fully hydraulic telescoping boom design mounted on a truck chassis. An Italian hydraulic-wheeled excavator designed by the Bruneri brothers surfaced in Italy in 1948. Lack of financial capital forced them to sell their patents to SICAM of France in 1954, enabling that firm to quickly introduce a truck-mounted hydraulic excavator of its own known as the Yumbo S25. Another French company, Poclain, built its own hydraulic excavator, the model TU, in 1951. All of these designs relied upon some sort of truck or wheeled chassis for locomotion. It was not until 1954 that the German company Demag introduced the world's first fully hydraulic excavator mounted on a crawler chassis capable of rotating a full 360 degrees. Identified as the Demag B504, this design layout eventually changed the face of earthmoving worldwide. Numerous manufacturers started to produce their own crawler-mounted hydraulic excavators.

Today, literally hundreds of companies around the world produce hydraulic excavators, but only a handful have designed machines that could be considered competition to the well-established large quarry and mining cable shovels. Most of these large hydraulic offerings have their origins in the United States, Germany, Japan, and France.

The large hydraulic excavator actually got its start with Poclain in France. That firm built its first truck-mounted loader in 1948 and its first "hydraulic" excavator in 1951. It was one of the leading European companies for most of the 1950s and

Liebherr R994B

In 2001, Liebherr introduced its upgraded R994B hydraulic mining excavator. Capacity of the R994B is rated at 23.5 cubic yards, with a power output of 1,502 flywheel horsepower. Operating weight is 326 tons. Shown working in June 2001 at Luzenac, France, is a backhoe version of the R994B. This unit was the second one built but was the first to be placed into service. The first R994B produced would not be delivered to SAMCA in Spain until September 2001. *Liebherr-France*

O&K RH300

The first hydraulic excavator to break the 500-ton operating-weight barrier was the O&K RH300. Weighing 549 tons, the RH300, with its 29-cubic-yard bucket, was the world's largest hydraulic excavator in its day. The first unit is shown here at O&K's Dortmund, Germany, plant in October 1979, wearing the colors of Northern Strip Mining Ltd. (NSM) of the United Kingdom. *Terex Mining*

1960s in the production of these types of machines. In 1970, the company unveiled a 10-cubic-yard hydraulic excavator, the EC 1000, at the Paris Expomat in France. Configured as a backhoe, the EC 1000 was the world's largest hydraulic excavator. Powered by three GM 8V-71 diesel engines, the EC 1000 boasted a total power output of 840 horsepower and had an operating weight of 151 tons. Up until that time, no other hydraulic excavator offered the capacity, power, or weight of the EC 1000. Not long after the introduction of the first EC 1000, a front shovel version fitted with an 11.5-cubic-yard bucket was released. Also at this time, power was increased slightly to 852 horsepower.

In the field, the EC 1000 machines performed quite well for such a groundbreaking design, though many thought the boxy design of the housing left a lot to be desired aesthetically. The reliability of the design of its hydraulic systems was called into question a number of times. Leaking high-pressure lines were a common complaint, but at the time, these were the best that could be built with the available machine tooling technology. As machine tools became more sophisticated and

precise, hydraulic cylinders could be machined to greater and more constant tolerances. Advances made in seal and high-pressure hose designs also increased the reliability of the breed. One has to remember that hydraulic systems of this size had never been built for a piece of earthmoving equipment that would be working in less than ideal conditions. Keeping the hydraulic fluid free of contaminants and maintaining a consistent viscosity of the fluid itself in extreme cold and hot climates were just two of the engineering hurdles that had to be addressed by Poclain, as well as every other manufacturer of these types of machines.

Lessons learned from the early EC 1000 machines led to an updated design with more muscle and a completely new look. Announced in late 1975 and released in 1976, the new model, now called the 1000 CK Series I, featured a totally new main housing that was compact and extremely elegant, just the reverse of the EC 1000. The new design weighed 179 tons and claimed a power output of 891 horsepower from only two Deutz diesel engines. Nominal bucket capacities ranged from 6.5 cubic yards for the backhoe and 11.5 for

O&K RH300

The first O&K RH300 was delivered into service in January 1980 at NSM's Donnington Extension Coal Mine in the United Kingdom. Power for the giant German shovel was supplied by two Cummins KTA2300-C1200 diesels, with a combined rating of 2,320 flywheel horsepower (2,400 gross). It is pictured at work in 1980 at the Donnington Extension. *Peter N. Grimshaw collection*

the front shovel. Only 10 of the original EC 1000 excavators had been built at the time of the introduction of the 1000 CK. This model line continued on with Poclain through the mid-1980s with many other improvements and upgrades. But by this time, other hydraulic excavator introductions from Germany and Japan had pushed it to the back of the class with repect to size. The 1000 series Poclains sold well in Europe, but only a handful were ever exported to North America.

Though the French had gotten a head start in the production of large hydraulic excavators, other European and Asian companies soon introduced designs of their own that eclipsed the big Poclains. Manufacturers such as O&K, Liebherr, Demag, and Hitachi all introduced machines in the 1970s that raised the industry bar for what was expected, both in performance and size, from a hydraulic design.

In 1975, Orenstein and Koppel of Germany, more commonly referred to as O&K, introduced its very popular model RH75. Weighing approximately 150 tons, it was about the same size as the original Poclain EC 1000. But that is where the similarity stopped. O&K was no stranger to building highly advanced hydraulic excavators, having

Bucyrus Erie 150-BD "Doubler"

The "Doubler" was Bucyrus Erie's attempt to combine the best engineering elements of a cable shovel with those of a hydraulic excavator. Designed with the assistance of Heckett Engineering Company of Illinois, the first Doubler front end was placed on an existing 150-B shovel located at Kaiser Steel Corporation's Eagle Mountain Mine in California in January 1968. The 150-BD was modified after testing and placed back into service in September of that year, now having been painted yellow. A second 150-BD was placed into testing in October 1969 at Hanna Mining Company's Butler Mine in Minnesota. Hanna Mining also operated the only 190-BD Doubler, built in early 1970. *Bucyrus International*

put its first fully hydraulic model, the RH5, into service in 1961. By the time the RH75 was put into production, more than 20,000 O&K hydraulic excavators of various sizes had been built and placed into service worldwide. The original RH75 was powered by two Cummins diesel engines that produced 840 horsepower combined. Nominal bucket capacity for the front shovel version was 10 cubic yards (5.25 for the backhoe). The RH75 was a compact and sleek design, especially when compared to the boxy Poclain EC 1000. In the field, the big O&K was a fast-cycling digging machine, with a fairly reputable reliability record. It was a winner from day one.

The Liebherr R991 was introduced in 1977. Liebherr, a Swiss-based, family-owned company with manufacturing plants located throughout the world, has been building hydraulic excavators since 1955, when it introduced a wheeled model called the L300. As the years passed, the company became known for its well-engineered hydraulic excavators. But with the introduction of the R991, Liebherr now had a machine that was a true large-production mining excavator that was well matched to the likes of the Poclain 1000 CK and

Above left: **Bucyrus Erie 550-HS**

Bucyrus Erie introduced its 550-HS hydraulic front shovel in 1982. Powered by a single Detroit Diesel 12V-92T engine, rated at 603 flywheel horsepower, the 140-ton 550-HS was capable of handling a standard 10-cubic-yard bucket. But because of the disastrous economic times of the world construction and mining markets in the early 1980s, Bucyrus Erie's hydraulic excavator program was ended in 1984, taking the 550-HS with it. Only two 550-HS shovels were listed as being built. *Author's collection*

Left: **Marion 3560**

Largest of the American-built hydraulic excavators from the 1980s was the Marion 3560. Introduced in 1981, the 3560 was powered by either two Caterpillar 3412PCTA diesel engines rated at 1,400 flywheel horsepower, or two Cummins VTA28-C725 diesels rated at 1,410 flywheel horsepower. Electric-powered versions were also available. Standard bucket capacity for the front shovel was 20 cubic yards. In 1988, an upgraded 3560B model was introduced weighing 307 tons in shovel form, carrying a standard 22-cubic-yard bucket. Production ended in 1989 with only eight units produced. *Author's collection*

O&K RH75. Weighing 182 tons, the R991 was right at the top of its class, with respect to size. The R991 was powered by two Cummins diesel engines, rated at 720 horsepower combined. Front-shovel bucket capacity was rated at 10 cubic yards (7 for backhoe), which put it in line with the rest of its competition. The Liebherr sold well in Europe and eventually was upgraded into a more powerful model known as the R992.

Not long after the introduction of the R991 by Liebherr came a response from one of the company's archrivals in Germany, Mannesmann Demag Baumaschinen. Demag let it be known that they were also going to introduce a hydraulic excavator of large proportions. Known as the Demag H241, the giant front shovel made its debut in 1978. For a short time, it was the world's largest hydraulic excavator. Weighing 310 tons, the H241 was far larger than anything the competition could put up against it. With a standard 19-cubic-yard bucket capacity, the big Demag was in a class all its own. Power was supplied by a single GM Detroit Diesel engine, with a maximum rating of 1,325 horsepower. With this capacity and available power, the H241 was capable of loading the typical 150-ton-payload hauler with five to six passes averaging 2.5 minutes. This kind of performance was squarely in the realm of the larger cable shovels. The Demag sold extremely well around the world and was one of the key machine designs that eventually pushed cable-type machines out of the 19- to 25-cubic-yard marketplace. The first production H241 found its home in North America at Benjamin Coal Company of Troutville, Pennsylvania. As time went by, the North American marketplace would become home to many more large Demag shovels.

The European manufacturers had complete dominance of the large hydraulic excavator marketplace throughout most of the 1970s. It was not until 1979 that the first large Japanese offering, the Hitachi UH801, was released. Many of the Japanese builders of hydraulic excavators had formed joint partnerships with various North

P&H 1200

P&H introduced its 1200 series hydraulic mining shovel in 1978. Originally engineered and built in Dortmund, Germany, manufacturing responsibilities eventually were shifted to the United States. The 1200 was rated as a 10.5-cubic-yard front shovel or an 8-cubic-yard backhoe. Power output was 860 flywheel horsepower, with an operating weight of 179 tons. *P&H Mining*

P&H 1200B

In February 1986, P&H placed its first 1200B excavator (pictured) into service at Magma Copper's San Manuel Mine in Arizona. Even though the power output was not changed from that of the previous 1200 model, it carried a larger 13-cubic-yard front shovel bucket. Its overall working weight had also increased to 208 tons. *P&H Mining*

American firms during the 1960s to share technical know-how, but more important, to give them access to American markets. By the mid-1970s, most of the larger Japanese firms wanted a larger presence in the North American marketplace and

more control over their offerings. As these firms released key models in the small- to medium-size range, it was only natural that a large quarry- or mining-type excavator would be introduced. Originally referred to as the UH80, the Hitachi UH801's size and performance output put it on a level playing field with the largest offerings at the time from Europe. The UH801's working weight of 173 tons was right in line with the largest offerings from Poclain and Liebherr. Power was supplied by two Cummins diesels with a combined flywheel rating of 800 horsepower (900 gross). Standard shovel bucket capacity was 11 cubic yards (10.25 for backhoe). The size of Hitachi's first big mining excavator made it suitable for medium and large quarry and mining operations. The UH801 was a favorite in coal mining operations in the United States, especially those east of the Mississippi River. The success of the UH801 opened the door for Hitachi's other large excavator offerings that soon followed, making the company one of the dominant players in the building of these types of machines.

Demag H485

The Demag H485 kicked the O&K RH300 off its throne as the world's largest hydraulic excavator. Introduced in 1986, the H485 was powered by a single MTU 16V-396TC43 diesel engine, rated at 2,103 flywheel horsepower. Equipped with a 30-cubic-yard bullclam, the first H485 was delivered to Coal Contractors, Ltd., for use at its Roughcastle site in Scotland. Weight was approximately 600 tons in full operating trim. *Author's collection*

Demag H485

In 1989, Demag delivered an electric-powered, 618-ton H485 front shovel to Boliden Mineral's Aitik copper mine near Gallivare, Sweden, equipped with a 34-cubic-yard bullclam. It was the fourth unit produced by Demag. Boliden liked the first H485 so much, they purchased another electric one just like it in 1991. The H485 shown is the first machine at work in May 1990. *Komatsu Mining*

Demag H485

Demag delivered its second H485 hydraulic front shovel to Klemke and Son Construction, Ltd., located north of Fort McMurray, Alberta, in 1989. Equipped with a 34-cubic-yard bullclam, the big Demag was used in the oil sands mining operations of the region. This H485 was the first to be powered by a 1,600-kilowatt (2,146-horsepower) electric motor. In early 1997, Klemke, which is now referred to as KMC Mining, sold its electric H485 to Suncor Energy. It is shown here at Suncor in October 1997. *ECO*

Demag H485
The fifth Demag H485 produced was the company's first backhoe version of its world-record-breaking hydraulic excavator. Weighing 618 tons equipped with a 34-cubic-yard bucket, it was built for Saxonvale Coal in Australia and delivered into service in February 1990. *Author's collection*

Liebherr R994
Largest of Liebherr's popular "Litronic" line of hydraulic excavators during the 1980s was its R994. Introduced in 1984, the R994 weighed approximately 230 tons equipped with a standard 17.6-cubic-yard bucket in front shovel form. Power was supplied by a single Cummins KTA38-C1050 diesel engine rated at 1,050 flywheel horsepower. By the mid-1990s, power was up to 1,125 flywheel horsepower, as was the weight at 250 tons for the shovel version. *Michael Hubert*

As the 1970s drew to a close, the large mining hydraulic excavator was slowly but surely making inroads into the marketplace. As large as these early designs were, especially the Demag H241, they were still not in the same league as the larger cable-type shovels. But by the end of 1979, a hydraulic machine was introduced by O&K that shattered all previous records for size for this type of excavator. Identified as the RH300, it was the first hydraulic excavator built to break the 500-ton operating weight class for a front shovel. The RH300 literally pushed the boundaries of what could be done technically and in terms of engineering for its day. And it was a great achievement, as well as risk, for O&K.

The first RH300 was unveiled at O&K's Dortmund factory on October 18, 1979. Previously, a preliminary 1:5-scale model of it was displayed at the American Mining Congress trade show in Las Vegas in 1978 to give the industry press a heads-up as to what was coming their way. The first unit was built for Northern Strip Mining (NSM) of the United Kingdom, for use at its Donnington Extension Coal Mine. The original RH300 was factory painted in the NSM colors of yellow, gray, and white, and was never painted in O&K red and gray. The massive RH300 weighed 549 tons in full operating trim. Standard bucket capacity was rated at 29 cubic yards. Power was supplied by two large Cummins KTA2300-C1200 supercharged and intercooled diesel engines, with a maximum output of 2,400 gross horsepower (2,320 flywheel).

The first RH300 was delivered into service in January 1980. Around 1981, NSM moved the big front shovel from its Donnington operations to its Godkine coal-mining facilities in Derbyshire. The first unit spent its entire working life with NSM, but RH300s built after this unit would not have it so easy in the marketplace. Just as the RH300 was establishing itself in the marketplace, the world economy entered a protracted recession. Sales of new mining equipment plummeted between 1981 and 1983. As planned mining expansions of the late 1970s were put on hold because of the uncertain times of the early 1980s, equipment manufacturers found themselves with large machines they could not sell. Unfortunately, the RH300 was one of these machines. That didn't mean O&K gave up on trying to sell the RH300. At the spring 1980 BAUMA trade exposition held in Munich, Germany, the company showed off the second RH300 to be built. Assembled to the same design specifications as the NSM machine, the BAUMA unit was painted in full O&K factory colors. The giant front shovel was the star of the show. But even with that, there were no orders placed for one. Eventually, the second unit was shipped back to the Dortmund factory for further testing. But soon

Hitachi EX3500

The Hitachi EX3500 was powered by two Cummins KT38-C925 diesel engines, rated at a combined 1,634 flywheel horsepower (1,760 gross). In late 2000, the EX3500 was replaced by the improved EX3600 series, capable of 1,880 flywheel horsepower, with a 27.5-cubic-yard bucket and a working weight of 386 tons. This gray EX3500 is working at the Lone Tree Gold Mine in Nevada in 1996. *ECO*

weeks became months, and then years, and still there was no buyer for the second RH300. The recession literally stopped O&K's large hydraulic excavator program dead in its tracks.

The third and last RH300 to be assembled was an electric version destined for a copper mine in Chile. Purchased by Codelco for use at its Chuquicamata mine, the electric RH300E was officially dedicated into service in mid-October 1987. The electric machine differed from the diesel-powered designs in several key areas: First, it was powered by two 900-kilowatt electric motors, giving the unit 2,414 horsepower to play with. Capacity had also been increased to 34 cubic yards. The operator now sat in a cab that was mounted higher for better visibility. The cab was painted light gray, while the cab on the BAUMA machine was painted red. All of these design changes pushed the weight of the RH300E up to 566 tons. One would like to say that all of these changes had made the RH300E the envy of the

mining industry. Unfortunately, the design age of the RH300 program was catching up with it. Though it worked for a few years in Chile, the electric RH300E was soon parked, never to work again. By the late 1980s, the RH300s were considered "dinosaurs" in the industry. What was cutting edge in 1979 was now yesterday's news. Eventually, the NSM machine was shut down and scrapped. The second unit was dismantled to supply parts to the other two operating shovels, and the electric model was permanently shut down in the early 1990s due to production slowdowns at the time. From the outside, it looks like the RH300 program was a failure for O&K. To a certain extent, it was. If the world economies had been in better shape, the story of the RH300 would have been vastly different. But the engineering knowledge gained from the three units by O&K engineers eventually enabled them to build a far more productive hydraulic mining excavator in the not too distant future.

SMEC 4500

Largest of the Japanese-built hydraulic excavators of the 1980s was the SMEC 4500, manufactured by Kobe Steel and Mitsubishi. The massive front shovel was conceived by the Surface Mining Equipment for Coal Technology Research Association (SMEC) of Japan, a joint partnership of 11 Japanese manufacturing companies. The 463-ton shovel is shown here during its dedication into service in November 1987 at BHP-Utah's Blackwater Mine, located in Queensland's Bowin Basin, Australia. *Les Kent*

SMEC 4500

The SMEC 4500 was powered by two diesel engines rated at 2,420 gross horsepower combined. Bucket capacity ranged from 19.6 to 39.2 cubic yards. Only one SMEC 4500 was ever built, and the shovel was scrapped in 1992 after the breakup of the SMEC group of companies because of liability concerns. *Les Kent*

O&K RH90C

O&K introduced its RH90C model in 1986. Weighing 179 tons, the RH90C was powered by a single Cummins KTA19-C525 diesel engine, rated at 844 flywheel horsepower (880 gross). The RH90C could be configured as a 13.1-cubic-yard front shovel, or a 11.6-cubic-yard backhoe. As of 2003, the excavator model is now referred to as the Terex TME90C (Terex Mining Excavator). This RH90C working in a European quarry in April 2002 is dropping a heavy steel "ball" on the larger stones in order to crush them. *Urs Peyer*

Meanwhile, back in North America, U.S. manufacturers were slow to respond to the larger classes of hydraulic excavators being introduced by their European and Asian counterparts during the 1970s. Most of the U.S. builders were well established in the business of designing and selling cable-type machines. But a few of these companies realized that the hydraulic excavator would ultimately spell the end to the contractor-sized cable shovels and backhoes. It was either a case of get on board or be left behind to the quickly evolving technology. Though many U.S. firms would eventually build and market hydraulic designs, only a handful took a chance on the larger quarry and mining machines. Most notable of these firms were Warner and Swasey of Solon, Ohio; Koehring, and P&H Harnischfeger, both of Milwaukee, Wisconsin; Northwest Engineering of Green Bay, Wisconsin; Bucyrus Erie of South Milwaukee, Wisconsin; and the Marion Power Shovel Company of Marion, Ohio. Not surprisingly, of these six companies, three were well established in the building of large electric cable shovels for the mining industry.

In 1972, Warner and Swasey introduced its Hopto 1900 hydraulic excavator. Configured as a backhoe, the 103-ton excavator was the largest hydraulic design produced by an American company up until that time. With 580 horsepower, the 1900 was at the top of its game working on large contracting jobs. But as big as the Hopto was, it still lacked the mass of a true big-production mining excavator.

The first U.S. firm to produce a hydraulic excavator specifically targeted for large quarry and mining operations was Koehring with its 130-ton Model 1266D from 1973. The company was well established in the manufacturing of these types of machines, having built its first fully hydraulic excavator, the 4-cubic-yard 505 Skooper, in 1963. The largest of the hydraulic designs to be built by the company was its 1466FS, first introduced in 1981. With a working weight of 154 tons and a standard bucket capacity of 10 cubic yards, the 898-flywheel-horsepower 1466FS front shovel was about the same size as the Poclain EC 1000. But then again, it did take the American company almost 10 years just to match the outdated French design, at least on paper. Production ended on the 1466FS in 1986.

In 1978, the long-respected builder of cable-type excavators, Northwest Engineering of Green Bay, Wisconsin, introduced a hydraulic mining shovel identified as the 65-DHS. Unique to this model was its "Transtick" design for the front-end attachment. Instead of using a boom and arm of fixed length, the Transtick design used a hydraulically extendable and retractable arm. This would allow the shovel to have a greater reach when needed by the operator at the touch of a button.

Above: **O&K RH200**

The O&K RH200 is the world's most popular mining excavator in the 500-tons-and-over category. Originally introduced in 1989, by the mid-1990s it was selling in numbers that were unheard of for an excavator weighing approximately 520 tons. This RH200 is working at Barrick Goldstrike in Nevada in September 1996 and was the second machine sold in the United States and the 46th unit sold overall. *ECO*

O&K RH200

The O&K RH200 standard bucket capacity for the front shovel in its early years was 26 cubic yards. This figure has increased steadily to 34 cubic yards. *ECO*

Above: **P&H 1550**

In 1989, P&H replaced its 1200B excavator model line with the new 1550 series. The 1550 was powered by a single Cummins KTTA 38C-1350 diesel engine rated at 1,100 flywheel horsepower. Standard bucket capacity for the front shovel was 15 cubic yards and 14 cubic yards for the backhoe. Average operating weight was 229 tons for the shovel and 225 tons for the backhoe. *P&H Mining*

Right: **P&H 2250**

P&H's largest hydraulic mining excavator series was its 2250. The first 2250 was formally introduced at the Electra 1990 mining exhibition at Johannesburg, South Africa, in September 1990. Power for the big 373-ton shovel was supplied by a single Caterpillar 3516 diesel engine rated at 1,800 flywheel horsepower. Standard bucket capacity was 23 cubic yards for the front shovel. Capacity for the 385-ton backhoe version was 22 cubic yards. *P&H Mining*

Rated at 5 to 6 cubic yards, the 456-horsepower, 107-ton shovel was over-engineered for its time. Though the model was also offered with a more conventional fixed front end, the 65-DHS could not find its way in the marketplace and was soon dropped from Northwest's product line. It would be the company's only real effort at building a completely hydraulic mining shovel. The company had been able to produce one of the all-time great cable-type shovels in the form of the 180-D. But building a viable hydraulic-type design was another matter entirely, one the company would never attempt again.

As for the top three manufacturers in the mining shovel world, Bucyrus Erie, Marion, and P&H all tried their hands at marketing hydraulic mining excavators during the 1970s and 1980s. Bucyrus Erie had been producing hydraulic machines since 1948, after it bought the Milwaukee Hydraulics Corporation, along with its Hydro-crane designs. In 1965, it released its first fully hydraulic design, the 20-H. Other models would follow, all of backhoe configuration. But all of these entries were contractor-sized machines, and none of them could be considered a true heavy mining excavator in the real sense.

In 1968, Bucyrus Erie did introduce a front shovel-type mining excavator that was a hybrid of both a cable and hydraulic design philosophy. Referred to as the "Doubler," it utilized cables to operate the boom and hydraulic cylinders to control the digging and dumping functions of the bucket. The front-shovel attachment was designed to fit the company's 150-B, 190-B, and 280-B shovel designs. The Doubler was a complicated design that promised greater productivity over a comparable cable-type machine. But it was a promise it could not deliver. In the end, only two 13-cubic-yard 150-BD (1968) and one 17-cubic-yard 190-BD (1970) Doublers were built. After the program was cancelled, the three field test shovels were returned to their original design configurations.

Bucyrus Erie's English subsidiary, Ruston-Bucyrus, produced a couple of smaller quarry hydraulic front shovel excavators, namely the 220-RS

P&H 2250 Series A

In late 1994, P&H introduced an upgraded version of its largest hydraulic excavator in the form of the 2250 Series A. The 2250A had its standard dipper capacity raised to 25 cubic yards, but most of the other changes centered around reliability and productivity improvements, such as a quad-turbocharged Caterpillar 3516 diesel replacing the previous dual-turbo setup, better computerized diagnostic systems, a new pump drive transmission, and an improved undercarriage. *P&H Mining*

Caterpillar 5230
Caterpillar introduced its largest hydraulic excavator, the 5230 series, in 1994. It would eventually be released in an updated 5230B form in November 2001. The 5230 series is rated at 22.2 cubic yards for the front shovel and weighs 361 tons. Power comes from a single Cat 3516B EUI diesel engine, rated at 1,550 flywheel horsepower (1,652 gross). *Keith Haddock*

and 375-RS, in 1980 and 1981, respectively. The first prototypes of the 220-RS were built in the late 1970s, and the 375-RS prototype was actually a converted Bucyrus Erie 350-H from 1979. But these were by no means in the same league as the larger German and Japanese offerings.

In 1981, Bucyrus Erie officially introduced its 500-H hydraulic excavator into the marketplace. Weighing 112 tons, it was a fairly robust machine for its day, at least by American manufacturing standards. The 500-H was rated at 9 cubic yards and was only available in a backhoe configuration. Right on the heels of the 500-H came the far larger 550-HS hydraulic front shovel in 1982. With a working weight of 140 tons, it was just a bit smaller than the Koehring 1466 FS, which came out the year earlier. The 550-HS was powered by a single 603-horsepower Detroit Diesel 12V-92T engine. Standard bucket capacity was rated at 10 cubic yards. The 550-HS and the 500-H were both extremely modern designs for their time, but these promising Bucyrus Erie designs never stood a chance in the marketplace during the 1980s' worldwide economic recession. As in most things, timing is everything. The story of these machines

would probably have ended differently if they had been developed a few years earlier. As it was, only nine of the 500-H and two 550-HS machines are listed as being produced before the company pulled the plug on their entire hydraulic excavator program in 1984.

Bucyrus Erie's closest rival, Marion Power Shovel, also tried its hand at designing and building a hydraulic excavator of its own. Since Marion did not already have an established hydraulic program in place at the time, it decided to focus strictly on the larger mining type of machine. And to simplify things even more, the new product line was limited to one model type offered in two working configurations. In 1981, Marion officially introduced its first hydraulic mining excavator, the 3560. The 3560 was designed from day one as a heavy-duty mining excavator. Originally released in a front shovel configuration, a large backhoe model would eventually be added to the product line. The big Marion was a robust-looking machine, clean of line, with no unnecessary clutter on the housing. Standard engine setup was two Caterpillar 3412PCTA diesel engines rated at 1,400 flywheel horsepower combined. In addition to the

Above: **Hitachi EX2500**
Hitachi introduced its "Super-EX" series EX2500 excavator in early 1996. Equipped with an 18.3-cubic-yard bucket and a working weight of 263 tons in shovel form, the EX2500 fits in the company's product line between the EX1900 and EX3600 excavators. This EX2500 at work in September 1996 at Santa Fe Pacific Gold Corporation's Lone Tree Mine in Nevada was the first EX2500 delivered into service in North America. *ECO*

Hitachi EX2500
Along with the front shovel version of the EX2500, Hitachi also offers a backhoe configuration. This version of the EX2500 uses an 18.1-cubic-yard bucket in standard form and weighs 260 tons. Power comes from a single Cummins KTA50-C diesel rated at 1,250 flywheel horsepower (1,300 gross). Pictured in October 1998 is P&M's EX2500 working at its Kemmerer Mine in western Wyoming. *ECO*

Liebherr R995

Liebherr released its R995 excavator model line in 1998. Weighing approximately 456 tons in shovel form, the R995 is a large machine, capable of handling a 30-cubic-yard bucket. Power output is listed at 2,140 flywheel horsepower from a single MTU 16V 4000E20 diesel engine. Pictured at the October 2000 MINExpo in Las Vegas, Nevada, is the first front shovel version of the R995 to be produced. *ECO*

Hitachi EX5500

Hitachi's EX5500 is powered by a pair of Cummins KTA50-C diesel engines, with a combined power output of 2,500 flywheel horsepower (2,600 gross). Weight of the EX5500 is 570 tons, either in shovel or backhoe form. This EX5500 backhoe working in a coal mine in Australia is equipped with a 38-cubic-yard bucket. *Urs Peyer*

diesel-engined unit, an electric version was also offered. Originally, the standard bucket capacity for the front shovel was 20 cubic yards (16 for backhoe), but as the design matured, that capacity was raised to 22 cubic yards (18 for backhoe). Early versions of the Marion weighed 300 tons for the front shovel and 312 tons for the backhoe, but the last machines built tipped the scales at 307 and 328 tons, respectively.

In the marketplace, the Marion 3560 was only a few tons lighter than the Demag H241 and, for its time, was the largest American-built hydraulic excavator on the market. But the big excavator shared the same fate as many other fine earthmoving machines introduced in the early 1980s.

Lack of customers and a shortage of development dollars hobbled the Marion hydraulic program. The company was just barely staying solvent in that tough recessionary time. On top of everything, the high costs of the SuperFront shovel program were also taking their toll on the company books. It soon became evident that the company had bitten off more than it could chew when it came to the hydraulic mining marketplace. In 1989, the company pulled the plug on the 3560 program as soon as the last two machines built, 23.5-cubic-yard barge-mounted 3560B backhoe dredges, were delivered to AOKI Marine Company of Japan. After this, Marion turned its back on hydraulic excavator production for good.

Hitachi EX5500

Hitachi introduced its giant "Super-EX" series EX5500 in July 1998. The first unit was delivered to North American Construction of northern Alberta, Canada, for an earthmoving contract at Syncrude's new Aurora Mine, located northeast of Mildred Lake. It is shown here in October 2001 loading a 320-ton-capacity Komatsu 930E with its 35.5-cubic-yard bullclam. *ECO*

The last of the big three mining shovel manufacturers to make room in its product line for hydraulic machines was P&H Harnischfeger. P&H had actually gained a fair amount of hydraulic design experience through a series of manufacturing joint partnerships and buyouts during the 1960s and 1970s. In 1964, P&H officially became a builder of hydraulic machines after it purchased the design rights to a small excavator built by the Cabot Corporation of Pampa, Texas. The first model type to be released by P&H was the H310 backhoe in 1965. Soon afterward, the H310 was followed up by the H312 and H418 model types, available only in backhoe form. These were eventually replaced, respectively, by the H-750 in 1974 and the H-1250 in 1975. From 1970 to 1974, P&H introduced larger excavators built under license from O&K. The largest of these releases was the 3.25-cubic-yard H-2500, which was based on the popular O&K RH25 design. None of these machines was in a size class for true hard-rock digging applications within a large mining operation.

Liebherr R996

As of 2003, the R996 Litronic is the largest hydraulic excavator model type offered by Liebherr. Officially introduced in May 1995, it is capable of using a standard 44.4-cubic-yard bullclam in front shovel form. Early versions of the R996 weighed approximately 603 tons, but today's model tips the scales at a healthy 700 tons. Shown at work in California in May 2002 is the first R996 to be placed into a mining operation in North America. *ECO*

Liebherr R996

Power for the Liebherr R996 is supplied by two large Cummins K1800E diesel engines, with a combined power rating of 3,000 flywheel horsepower (3,600 gross). With its large 44.4-cubic-yard bucket, the R996 can make the toughest digging jobs look easy. *ECO*

In 1978, P&H introduced its new 1200 model series. Originally released in front shovel form, and then a backhoe version in 1979, the 1200 was a German-engineered design built in Dortmund, Germany. But as the series matured, manufacturing responsibilities for the line were shifted to the United States. The 1200 weighed approximately 179 tons in front shovel or backhoe configurations, which was right in line with other popular European hydraulic mining shovels of the day. The standard rock bucket for the front shovel version was rated at 10.5 cubic yards. Standard backhoe capacity was 8 cubic yards. Power was supplied by two diesel engines with a combined power rating of 860 flywheel horsepower. Reliability issues, along with a host of mechanical upgrades, were addressed in a 1200B, which was

first released in front shovel form in February 1986. The 1200B had the same power output as its predecessor, but the standard bucket capacity was now rated at 13 cubic yards, with an approximate working weight of 208 tons. Though the 1200/1200B series sold well enough throughout the 1980s, they were not in the same class with respect to sales as their counterparts from O&K, Demag, and Hitachi. P&H did propose a significantly larger hydraulic machine in 1983 in the form of the 393-ton model 2200. But the stagnant business climate of the day kept potential customers on the sidelines. In the end, no 2200 ever made it into iron. But the basic design parameters of the big hydraulic excavator proposal would eventually become a reality for the company in the 1990s, not as the 2200, but instead as the model 2250.

Liebherr P996

Along with land-based R996 excavators, Liebherr also offers a barge-mounted dredge version identified as the P996. The pontoon P996 excavator shown here at work in 2001, on the construction of the "South Valley Project" irrigation system in Upper Egypt, is equipped with an 82-foot-long gooseneck boom, a 39-foot 4-inch stick, and a 7.5-cubic-yard-capacity bucket for dredging. *Liebherr-France*

As the 1980s progressed, U.S. companies played a game of catch-up with their European counterparts, who, for their part, just kept on introducing hydraulic excavators of larger and larger proportions. The largest of all of these designs during this time period was the Demag H485. Released in 1986, it capped off an amazing year for the company that also saw it introduce a larger model than its H241 identified as the H285. With a payload capacity of 18.5 cubic yards and a working weight of 329 tons, the H285 was a true heavyweight for a hydraulic shovel or backhoe. But it paled in comparison to its larger brother, the H485. Simply put, the H485 became the world's largest hydraulic excavator at the time of its introduction. Weighing a staggering 600 tons in full operating trim, it bested the previous record holder, the O&K RH300, by some 51 tons. Bucket capacity was also enormous for its time, with a standard 31-cubic-yard rating for the prototype machine and 34 cubic yards for units that followed it out of the factory. Power for the giant was supplied by a single MTU 16V-396TC43 diesel engine rated at 2,103 flywheel horsepower. Other variations of the H485 included a 34-cubic-yard backhoe model, as well as an electric-powered version.

Sales were encouraging for such a large hydraulic machine in a market that was just coming out of some very difficult times. While sales of the RH300 suffered because of the timing of its release, the opposite was true for the H485. It was able to survive by being introduced into the marketplace just as big mining operations around the world were adding new equipment to meet the demands of the improved economic conditions. The H485 sold well throughout the rest of the 1980s, as did its little brother, the H285, which sold in numbers that surprised many in the mining industry.

Liebherr was also expanding its hydraulic lines in the 1980s with the introduction of the R994 in 1984 and the R992 in 1986. The R992 was a 157-ton, 800-flywheel-horsepower excavator equipped with a standard bucket capacity of 12 cubic yards. The larger R994 weighed 230 tons, with a power output of 1,050 flywheel horsepower. Its standard bucket capacity was rated at 17.6 cubic yards. Both were also available in backhoe configurations. Liebherr's largest hydraulic models sold extremely well throughout the rest of the 1980s and well into the 1990s, setting the company up for even larger models to follow.

The 1980s was also a good time for Japanese manufacturers as well. Hitachi made great strides in engineering during this time period, culminating with the release of a whole new generation of "GIANT-EX" series of mining excava-

Demag H285S

In 1986, Demag replaced its H241 excavator with the improved H285 series. The H285 was equipped with a standard 18.5-cubic-yard bucket and was power rated at 1,500 flywheel horsepower. Overall working weight was 329 tons. In 1992, the model was released in an upgraded H285S form. The H285S shovel featured a 25-cubic-yard bullclam, a power rating of 1,675 flywheel horsepower (1,750 gross), and an overall operating weight of 369 tons. *Komatsu Mining*

Komatsu PC4000

In late 1999 the H285S became the Komatsu PC4000. The PC4000 featured an all-new cab design, as well as an increase in power to 1,875 gross horsepower. Standard shovel bucket capacity is 28 cubic yards, with the backhoe version coming in at 29 cubic yards. Standard working weight was now up to 408 tons for the front shovel and 420 tons for the backhoe configuration. This PC4000 backhoe is working in an Australian coal mine in March 2002. *Urs Peyer*

Demag H455S
Introduced in 1995, the Demag H455S is a 33-cubic-yard hydraulic excavator that is in direct competition with O&K's very popular RH200 series. Power comes from two Cummins KTTA38-C diesels, rated at 2,144 flywheel horsepower (2,250 gross). Pictured at Boliden Mineral's Apirsa zinc mine in Aznalcollar, Spain, is the 540-ton prototype machine, an electric-powered unit rated at 1,700 kilowatts (2,280 horsepower). In late 1999 the H455S was renamed the Komatsu PC5500.
Komatsu Mining

tors in 1987. The largest of these were the EX1800 and EX3500. The 193-ton EX1800 was a 13.5-cubic-yard machine, with a power output of 920 flywheel horsepower, ideal for large quarry operations. The EX3500 was a much brawnier machine than the EX1800. With a working weight of 362 tons, a bucket capacity of 23.5 cubic yards, and power of 1,660 flywheel horsepower, it had the credentials to go with its size. From the start, both of Hitachi's big entries in the marketplace were big successes in the mining industry worldwide, including the all very important U.S. market. The Hitachi machines were very competitively priced at the time and made the European offerings a bit expensive looking for some operations. The EX3500 sold in numbers never before seen for its weight class, and its sales success continued well into the 1990s.

Another large Japanese hydraulic excavator of the 1980s was the SMEC 4500. This massive shovel was conceived by the Surface Mining Equipment for Coal Technology Research Association (SMEC) of Japan, which was a joint partnership of 11 Japanese manufacturers whose purpose was to design large mining equipment to meet Japan's future mineral and energy needs. The SMEC 4500 was jointly designed by Mitsubishi Heavy Industries and Kobe Steel and was fabricated at Kobe's Takasago Works. The specifications of the hybrid hydraulic shovel were impressive for its day: 2,420 gross horsepower, capacity range of 19.6 to 39.2 cubic yards, and a working weight of 463 tons, all put the SMEC 4500 in the upper echelon of giant hydraulic machines. The prototype unit was put into trial service in November 1987 at BHP-Utah's Blackwater Mine in Queensland's Bowin Basin, Australia, and was officially handed over to the mine in March 1988 as ready for duty. But after the breakup of the companies that formed the joint venture in the early 1990s, it was decided to scrap the project for liability reasons in 1992. Only one of these giants ever saw the light of day.

Another one-off giant hydraulic shovel of the 1980s was the Russian-built Uralmash EG-20. But like so many other Soviet-era machines, the electric-powered EG-20 was a bit over-engineered. Weighing 507 tons, with a bucket capacity of 26 cubic yards, the Russian design was big and extremely complex. Though the upper works was electric powered, the undercarriage was mechanically driven. Working power output was listed at 1,690 horsepower. It was eventually delivered into service in late 1985 at the Kemeroro coal mine in Kuzbass. But in the end, only one of these giant Russian shovels was ever built.

The company that seemed to get the most out of the 1980s concerning engineering and production was O&K. Though the massive RH300 was a major disappointment for the company, it did not keep them from launching new model lines with state-of-the-art technology. One of the company's greatest contributions to the evolution of the hydraulic shovel was its development of "TriPower" linkage, which helped keep the digging geometry of the bucket at a constant position throughout the digging cycle, giving the machine up to 50 percent greater crowd force than its nearest rivals. Tested throughout 1981 at various mining and

Demag H485S

Demag placed its first H485 hydraulic excavator into the United States in August 1993 at Magma Copper Company's Pinto Valley Mine in Miami, Arizona. An electric version, the H485SE, was rated at 2,100 kilowatts (2,850 horsepower) and equipped with a 44-cubic-yard bullclam. Its service operating weight tipped the scales at 705 tons. In late November 1994 the shovel was moved to a new location at ASARCO's Ray complex, near Hayden, Arizona. In 1997 it was sold to Reading Anthracite Company in Pottsville, Pennsylvania. The H485SE is pictured here operating at ASARCO in September 1996. *ECO*

Below: **Demag H685SP**

In March 1995, Demag delivered a special H685SP front shovel to Klemke and Son Construction, just north of Fort McMurray, Alberta. The H685SP is powered by a pair of Caterpillar 3516DI-TA diesel engines with a combined power output of 3,730 flywheel horsepower (4,000 gross). Here, it is preparing for work in the oil sands after completing all of its on-site assembly testing requirements. *Gary Middlebrook*

Demag H685SP

The Demag shovel purchased by Klemke, now referred to as KMC Mining, carries the designation of H685SP. After the launch of the machine, Demag decided to change the product line's nomenclature to H485SP. But since the first H685SP was already in service, the nomenclature of that machine was not changed. Thus, it is the only machine to carry the H685SP description. It is shown here loading a 240-ton-capacity Caterpillar 793B hauler in 2001. *Keith Haddock*

quarry operations in Europe, it was officially introduced into the marketplace in 1982 with the newly redesigned RH40C.

The TriPower system showed up next on one of the company's finest designs, the RH120C. Introduced at the 1983 BAUMA trade show in Germany, the RH120C was an instant hit with mining operations the world over. Weighing 232 tons, the excavator was positioned in one of the most competitive classes of machines. But with 1,200 gross horsepower and a 15.7-cubic-yard bucket, the RH120C had nothing to apologize for. And with the aid of its TriPower design, it quickly became the standard by which all other hydraulic excavators in this size class were judged.

In 1986, O&K introduced another new excavator design called the RH90C; it was sized in between the RH75C and RH120C. Weighing 179 tons, with a 13.1-cubic-yard bucket and 880 flywheel horsepower, the RH90C soon proved itself in the field as one incredibly tough digging machine. And like all of the other big O&K offerings, it was available in electric and backhoe configurations.

O&K brought the decade to a close with the release of what would become one of the mining industry's most popular large hydraulic excavators to date, the incredible RH200. Introduced at the

1989 BAUMA exposition in Munich, Germany, the RH200 was a little bit smaller than an RH300. The original RH200 weighed 441 tons in full operating trim, but later units carried more in the neighborhood of 529 tons, just 20 tons shy of the original RH300. Power output was listed at 2,100 flywheel horsepower, with a bucket capacity of 26 cubic yards. But, as with the weight, these figures also rose as the years rolled by. The first RH200 was delivered into service to Budge Mining, West Chevington, Northumberland, in the United Kingdom in May 1989. Budge had been a longtime buyer of large O&K machines and was eager to put the RH200 through its paces. Company executives were so impressed with the performance of the big O&K that they ordered a second RH200 in November of that same year.

For manufacturers in the United States, the production and marketing of successful large-scale hydraulic mining excavators had not gone as planned. In fact, only P&H was able to enter the 1990s with hydraulic designs that could be considered true hard-rock digging machines. In 1989, the company replaced its 1200B model with the 229-ton 1550 series. The 1550 boasted 1,100 flywheel horsepower from a single Cummins diesel engine and a standard bucket capacity of 15 cubic

yards. P&H released an even larger machine in 1990, the 2250. Weighing 373 tons, the 2250 was comparable in size to some of the most popular hydraulic excavators available to the mining market. Its standard bucket capacity rating of 23 cubic yards also made it capable of loading 150- to 200-ton haul trucks quickly and efficiently. Power was supplied by a single Caterpillar 3516 diesel engine rated at 1,800 flywheel horsepower. In 1994, an improved 2250 Series A was introduced, which included improvements to address reliability and production issues. Standard bucket capacity was

Demag H685SP

The Demag H685SP is equipped with a 46-cubic-yard bullclam, capable of handling a 70-ton payload. Its overall working weight is 755 tons. Shown here working hard in October 1997, the big Demag takes another 70-ton bite of overburden while working on an earthmoving contract at Syncrude's base mine. *ECO*

Komatsu-Demag H655S

In May 1998, Komatsu-Demag placed its first H655S hydraulic front shovel into service at BHP's Ekati Diamond Mine in the Northwest Territories. Designed as a replacement for the H485S, the H655S featured a redesigned front end. Power came from two Caterpillar 3516DI-TA diesels, rated at 3,714 flywheel horsepower (3,728 gross). Standard bucket capacity was 46 cubic yards, with an overall working weight of 755 tons. At the end of 1999, this model line was renamed the Komatsu PC8000. *Komatsu Mining*

Komatsu-Demag H740 OS

The Komatsu-Demag H740 OS is a specially designed hydraulic shovel built for KMC Mining (Klemke). Built for abrasive oil sands work, it features a wider car body, three swing transmissions, wider track pads, and parallel linkage. Power output is set at 4,400 gross horsepower, with an operating weight of 815 tons. Bucket capacity is 52.3 cubic yards. The H740 OS went into service in January 1999. *Keith Haddock*

now listed at 25 cubic yards. By this time, P&H was starting to feel the financial strain of fielding its hydraulic mining excavators. Though the company continued to promote the 1550 and 2250A shovels and backhoes through 1996, it became apparent that no one was really listening in the marketplace. In the end, the company quietly ended production on the two designs, and as soon as its inventory of built machines was sold, closed its books on the production of hydraulic mining excavators in Milwaukee.

Caterpillar, on the other hand, found the decade more to its liking when it came to hydraulic mining machines. Although it had been producing hydraulic excavators since 1972, Caterpillar had never offered a design that could be compared to some of the larger entries in the field available from Europe and Japan. That all changed in October 1992, when the company unveiled its first hydraulic mining front shovel, the 5130, at the American Mining Congress show, held in Las Vegas, Nevada. The 5130 was designed from the

ground up as a heavy-duty mining excavator and was not just some existing machine platform that had been "beefed up" or modified. The 5130 was, in fact, the first in a new product line of 5000 series mining shovels and mass excavators the company was about to release throughout the 1990s. The original 188-ton 5130 was powered by a single Cat 3508 diesel, rated at 755 flywheel horsepower. Standard bucket capacity was listed at 13.75 cubic yards. In 1993, a backhoe mass excavator (ME) configuration was added to the mix, equipped with a general-purpose 13-cubic-yard bucket. As the 5130 product line matured, it was fed a steady diet of upgrades and improvements that raised its operating weight up to 193 tons by 1995. In 1997, an improved 5130B model was introduced. Power had now been increased to 800 flywheel horsepower, as had the bucket capacity, with the front shovel now rated at 14.5 cubic yards, and the ME at 13.7 cubic yards. Operating weight was now up to 200 tons. The 5130B would continue on through 2002 with these same operating specifications.

The largest hydraulic excavator offered by Caterpillar is its 5230 series. Originally announced in 1993, the first machine was officially put into the field in 1994. Weighing 347 tons with a bucket capacity of 22.2 cubic yards, the 5230 clearly had the Hitachi EX3500's market in its sights. The big excavator was powered by a single Cat 3516 diesel, rated at 1,470 flywheel horsepower. In 1995, Caterpillar added a 20.3-cubic-yard mass excavator to round out the 5230 line. In the field, the big Cat performed well for such a new design. As with the original 5130 series, the 5230 had its share of reliability concerns and mishaps. But with the massive Cat dealership network to back the machines up, problems were quickly identified and corrected. It was not long before the 5230 claimed dominance in mining industry sales of its size

Terex O&K RH200

The Terex O&K RH200 is just about as perfect as a hydraulic mining excavator can be. Today's machine is equipped with a standard 34-cubic-yard bucket in front shovel form. For the backhoe configuration, 27.6 cubic yards is the norm. Overall working weight is 529 tons. White with red stripes is now the current Terex Mining corporate color scheme. *ECO*

Terex O&K RH200

The Terex O&K RH200 is powered by two Cummins KTA38C-1200 diesel engines, rated at 2,102 flywheel horsepower (2,400 gross). For mining operations requiring an electric machine, the RH200 can be fitted with a single 1,600-kilowatt electric motor. Pictured in June 2000 at work in a coal mine in the Powder River Basin of Wyoming is a diesel-powered version of the RH200. Starting in 2003, the RH200 is now being referred to as the Terex TME200. *ECO*

Terex Mining updated the RH120C, which had been on the market since 1983, with the new Terex O&K RH120E in October 1999. The RH120E (renamed the TME120E in 2003) was powered by a single Cummins QSK19-C diesel, rated at 1,280 flywheel horsepower (1,500 gross), and has an operating weight of 292 tons. Bucket capacity is listed at 19.6 cubic yards for either a shovel or backhoe configuration. This RH120E backhoe is at work in May 2002 at Schwenk Cement in Allmendingen, Germany. *Urs Peyer*

class. In 2001, Caterpillar released an upgraded 5230B version of its popular mining excavator. The operating weight was now up to 361 tons, and the power output had increased to 1,550 flywheel horsepower. Bucket capacities remained fairly similar to that of the original model, with the mass excavator up just a bit to 21 cubic yards for the rock bucket. As of 2003, the Caterpillar line of hydraulic mining excavators are the only such machines designed and built by an American company in North America.

Even though Caterpillar had made great sales gains over its rivals at Hitachi concerning the big hydraulic excavators, the Japanese company countered with new and improved model designs throughout the 1990s and into the next century. In 1991, the company introduced its "Super-EX" mining machines, which featured improved reliability and performance upgrades. For the EX1800, its operating weight and bucket capacity were up to 199 tons and 13.7 cubic yards, respectively, but power was now listed at 900 flywheel horsepower (1,000 gross) due to new ratings standards. As for

the EX3500, it saw its weight top off at 368 tons, but bucket capacity remained unchanged. Power ratings were now 1,634 flywheel horsepower (1,760 gross), again due to new ratings standards. In 1996, Hitachi introduced the "Super-EX" series EX2500 model line. Weighing 263 tons, the EX2500 was designed to fit in between the EX1800 and EX3500 in the company's product line. Powered by a single 1,250-flywheel-horsepower (1,300 gross) Cummins diesel engine, the EX2500 is able to handle an 18.3-cubic-yard bucket in front shovel form and 18.1 in backhoe configuration.

At the 2000 MINExpo in Las Vegas, Hitachi announced the release of an improved version of its popular EX3500 identified as the EX3600. Weighing 386 tons, the new EX3600 has a power output of 1,880 flywheel horsepower with a standard front shovel bucket capacity of 27.5 cubic yards. In 2001, the company also improved its EX1800, making it the EX1900. At 205 tons, 1,025 flywheel horsepower, and a 14.4-cubic-yard capacity, the new EX1900 was superior to its predecessor in all areas were it counts.

O&K RH400 11-35

In October 1997, O&K introduced its incredible RH400 mining front shovel. With a bucket capacity of 55 cubic yards, an 80-ton payload, and a working weight of 910 tons, it was the world's largest hydraulic excavator. Power for the behemoth was provided by two Cummins K2000E diesels, rated at 3,350 flywheel horsepower (4,000 gross) combined. Pictured at Syncrude's Base Mine in 1997 is the first RH400, carrying Syncrude shovel number 11-35. *ECO*

O&K RH170

The O&K RH170 was originally introduced in 1995 as a 23.5-cubic-yard mining excavator. The RH170 is powered by two Cummins KT38-C98 diesels, rated at 1,662 flywheel horsepower (1,850 gross), with a service weight of 397 tons. A 22.9-cubic-yard backhoe version is also available. In 2003, the RH170 was renamed the Terex TME170. *Terex Mining*

But the largest of all Hitachi's mining excavators as of 2002 was its Giant Super-EX series EX5500. First introduced in 1998, it was the largest hydraulic excavator ever to come out of Japan, beating out the previous Japanese record holder, the SMEC 4500. The EX5500's working weight of 570 tons put it in direct competition with the leader in this weight category, the O&K RH200. Wielding a 35.5-cubic-yard bucket (38-cubic-yard backhoe) with 2,500 flywheel horsepower (2,600 gross) from two Cummins diesels to back it up, the EX5500 is a stellar performer in the mining industry. With only a few years of production under its belt, Hitachi's top-of-the-line excavator has found great acceptance in mining operations in Canada, Australia, and the United States.

During the last decade of the 20th century, European manufacturers were also lining up ultra-large hydraulic excavator releases of their own that would eventually dwarf anything built in the United States or Japan. One of these was Liebherr. That company continued its sales success in the mining industry by building on what it had achieved with its R991/R992/R994 model releases. In 1997, the company announced the introduction of a new R995 model line, but it was not until late 1998 that the first unit (a backhoe configuration) was delivered into service in Spain. The R995 weighed 456 tons, with a power output of 2,140 flywheel horsepower and a standard bucket capacity of 30 cubic yards—rock-solid numbers no matter how you looked at them. In 2001, the company released an improved R994B model, which now claimed a working weight of 326 tons, power of 1,502 flywheel horsepower, and a bucket capacity of 23.5 cubic yards. Far larger than the previous R994, the new "B" model is well positioned in the marketplace to take on future mining expansions expected in the first decade of the new century.

Largest of all the Liebherr excavator designs is its R996. Introduced in 1995, it is one of the standout designs in its size class in the industry. Only a few hydraulic machines today can best its 700-ton working weight (603 tons for prototype unit), let alone its standard bucket capacity of 44.4 cubic yards. The R996 gets its power from two Cummins K1800E diesels with a combined rating of 3,000 flywheel horsepower (3,600 gross). The biggest of all Liebherrs can be configured as a front shovel or backhoe. As for sales of the two types, the backhoe model with a 39.2-cubic-yard bucket is the most preferred, especially for the units working in Australia. The R996 upper works can also be

adapted for marine work when mounted on a barge for dredging purposes and is considered the largest barge-mounted hydraulic excavator in the world.

The 1990s was a time of change for Mannesmann Demag and its broad range of hydraulic mining excavators. In November 1995, Demag signed an agreement with Komatsu, Ltd. to form a new 50-50 joint venture company to be called Demag-Komatsu GmbH. During this time, excavators were built and sold throughout the world carrying the Demag-Komatsu name. In February 1999, Komatsu agreed to purchase 100 percent ownership in the joint venture, giving the Japanese company complete control over the German-designed-and-built excavators. This company is now known as Komatsu Mining Germany GmbH. As for the Demag name, it is no longer used in conjunction with the production of excavators of any kind.

During this time, Demag and Komatsu introduced many new model types and model-type nomenclature by the end of 1999. In 1997, Demag-Komatsu introduced the 265-ton H255S, which

replaced the H185S in the product line. In late 1999, the H255S became the PC3000. At this point, the PC3000 was merely a rebadged H255S. But in 2001, improvements were introduced that raised its standard bucket capacity from 18.3 to 19.5 cubic yards and raised the working weight to 285 tons.

Next in size to the H255S/PC3000 in Demag's product line was the popular H285 series, which would become the 369-ton H285S in 1992. In late 1999, it would become the PC4000. The first PC4000 to be introduced into the field with a new cab design was in 2000. Along with the cab, the new design had an increased working weight of 425 tons, with a bigger bucket of 28 cubic yards (25 for the H285S). Power was listed at 1,875 gross horsepower.

After the H285S/PC4000 came the H455S. Originally announced in 1994, the first unit was not delivered into service until mid-1995. And as with previous models in the product line, it was renamed in 1999, becoming the PC5500 late in that year. In 2000, the first PC5500 with an improved cab design was placed into service. The

O&K RH400 11-37

In April 2000, Syncrude placed the first of two new O&K RH400 front shovels into operation that were purchased for its new Aurora Mine site. These shovels featured many improvements over the original two units, including a longer boom, new undercarriages, raised cabs, larger 56.9-cubic-yard buckets, and two big powerful Caterpillar 3516B diesel engines, rated at 4,400 flywheel horsepower (4,600 gross). Here, Syncrude's Aurora RH400 11-37 is loading a 320-ton-capacity Komatsu 930E in October 2001. *ECO*

O&K RH400 11-37
All of the improvements made to the latest Syncrude RH400 shovels working at its Aurora Mine raised their operating weights up to 985 tons, another record for a hydraulic excavator. *ECO*

H455S/PC5500 both weigh 540 tons, with identical standard bucket capacities of 33 cubic yards. The biggest difference between the two, except for the new cab design in the later machines, was an increase in power from 2,250 to 2,520 gross horsepower.

At the top of the Demag excavator food chain was its H485 design. This legendary machine became the H485S in 1992. The 705-ton H485S had a larger bucket capacity of 44 cubic yards, as well as an increased power output of 3,590 gross horsepower (3,000 flywheel). In 1995, a special edition of this model line was delivered to Klemke Mining Corporation in Fort McMurray, Alberta, Canada. Identified as the H685SP, it was a heavier and

more powerful version of the H485S. The H685SP tipped the scales at 755 tons, with a bucket capacity of 46 cubic yards and an engine output of 4,000 gross horsepower (3,730 flywheel). After delivery of the unit, Demag decided to change the nomenclature of the design to H485SP. But Klemke liked the idea of owning the only H685SP in existence, so the designation was left as-is on their machine.

The giant Demag continued to evolve throughout the late 1990s. In May 1998, the first H655S was put to work. Weighing 755 tons, with a 46-cubic-yard bucket and a 3,728-gross-horsepower (3,714-flywheel) rating, it featured an improved boom design not found on the H485S/SP. In January 1999, another special edition of the big

shovel was delivered into service for Klemke Mining. This one-of-a-kind machine called the H740 OS had many structural design improvements incorporated into it. This helped it cope with the extreme digging conditions that it would encounter in the oil sand operations of Northern Alberta. The H740 OS is equipped with a 52.3-cubic-yard bucket and has a power rating of 4,400 gross horsepower. In full operating trim, the giant front shovel weighs 815 tons, the most for any of the H485-series-derived machines.

By the end of 1999, the H655S became the Komatsu PC8000. The first unit to carry the PC8000 nomenclature was delivered into Western Australia in late 1999. But this version was identical in specifications to the H655S. It was not until early 2003 that the improved PC8000 design was actually built and delivered to a customer. The new PC8000 featured a redesigned operator's cab and was powered by two Komatsu SDA16V160 diesel engines, rated at 4,020 gross horsepower combined. A version powered by two electric motors can also be specified and is capable of producing output of 2,900 kilowatts, or 3,889 horsepower. Operating weight of the PC8000 in front shovel form is 788 tons, with the backhoe version coming

in at a healthy 800 tons. Standard bucket capacity is rated at 50 cubic yards. The first three of the new PC8000 excavators were delivered to CVRD in Brazil, which also operates a fleet of seven older H485 units. All 10 machines are electric-powered front shovels.

Life in the 1990s for O&K was not all that different from Demag's. Larger mining excavators continued to be introduced, and the company went through some rather dramatic changes in ownership. In December 1997, Orenstein and Koppel Aktiengesellschaft announced that it would sell its large mining excavator division, O&K Mining GmbH, to Terex Mining Equipment, Inc., a division of Terex Corporation. By early 1998 the deal was complete. O&K Mining was now part of the Terex group, in a new division simply referred to as Terex Mining, headquartered in Tulsa, Oklahoma. Though the mining excavator product lines are now owned by Terex, all of the manufacturing for them is still carried out at the Dortmund, Germany, facilities.

As the new century began, the RH200 still reigned supreme in the mining world as the best-selling hydraulic excavator in the 500-plus-ton class, with more than 84 units sold by the end of

O&K RH400 11-38
The second RH400 to be placed in service at Syncrude's Aurora Mine was shovel 11-38, in May 2000. The RH400 11-38 was identical to 11-37 in capacity, power, and weight. It is pictured here loading a 386-ton-capacity Caterpillar 797 hauler in June 2001. *Keith Haddock*

Terex O&K RH400E

In July 2000, Terex Mining placed its first Terex O&K RH400 into service in the United States. An electric-powered RH400E, it was delivered to Kennecott Energy's Jacobs Ranch Mine in the Powder River Basin, located south of Gillette, Wyoming. In May 2001, over a three-week period, the electric front shovel was moved over to Kennecott's Antelope Mine, also in the PRB. *Michael Hubert*

2002. Though the RH200 can be found working in all of the key mining regions of the world, Australia and South Africa have the largest number of units in the field. Today's RH200 weighs 529 tons and has a power output of 2,102 flywheel horsepower. Bucket capacity has slowly crept up over the years and is now rated at 34 cubic yards. Other than a color change from red to white after the Terex acquisition, the RH200 continues into this century virtually unchanged.

Another one of O&K's star excavator designs has also made an enviable name for itself in the marketplace. Since its introduction in 1983, the RH120C has been a market leader in its size class. In October 1999, Terex Mining released an updated version of its best seller, the RH120E. Simply put, the RH120E is a more powerful and heavier version of the older "C" model. Weighing 292 tons, with 1,280 flywheel horsepower on tap, and a 19.6-cubic-yard bucket, it is about as perfect as a mining excavator can get in its size class.

And the popular Terex O&K machine has the sales numbers to back it up. By the end of 2002, more than 244 units of the RH120C/E model types had been sold worldwide.

The 1990s also saw O&K add a new model type sized between its popular RH200 and RH120C series excavators called the RH170. Weighing 397 tons, the RH170 was certainly big. And with 1,662 flywheel horsepower and a 23.5-cubic-yard standard bucket rating, it could take on all contenders in its weight class. Officially unveiled at the April 1995 BAUMA mining show in Germany, it is currently available in front shovel and backhoe configurations. When it became a Terex machine in 1998, about the only noticeable change was a new white paint job with red striping.

O&K introduced one more major excavator before the Terex acquisition, and what a release it was. Identified as the RH400, it was literally the world's largest hydraulic excavator. Built for Syncrude Canada, the RH400 was designed

Terex O&K RH400E
The Terex O&K RH400E is powered by two electric motors, generating a combined 3,200 kilowatts (4,291 horsepower). This gives the RH400E exceptional cycle times and the power to dig in the hardest conditions. Overall working weight is 976 tons. Pictured is the RH400E operating at Kennecott Energy's Antelope Mine in September 2002. *ECO*

for working in the extremely abrasive oil sand operations north of Fort McMurray, Alberta. In the types of working conditions that the excavator could encounter, only the largest and most powerful front shovel would do. And here, the RH400 did not disappoint. The mammoth hydraulic shovel was designed and built over an 18-month period starting in 1995. Engineering teams both from O&K and Syncrude were brought together to jointly develop key design areas of the shovel to ensure it would meet the rigorous demands of digging in the oil sands. In July 1997, the first unit, wearing Syncrude machine number 11-35, was unveiled at the O&K Dortmund facilities. After additional testing of the RH400's components were completed at the factory, the unit was shipped in August to its new home in Canada. By early October, the first RH400 was assembled and deemed ready for action.

On October 22, 1997, the RH400 was officially dedicated into service. Weighing 910 tons in full operating trim, the giant O&K was far larger than any hydraulic excavator then on the market from any manufacturer. Up front, the RH400 was equipped with a 55-cubic-yard bucket, capable of handling an 80-ton payload. Power for the behemoth was supplied by two Cummins K2000E diesels rated at 3,350 flywheel horsepower (4,000 gross) combined. As powerful as these engines were, the RH400 was actually designed for Cummins's new QSK60 powerplants. But the development of the excavator itself was running ahead of that of the engines. In time, the original engines would be replaced with the more powerful QSK60 type. After a few unforeseen reliability issues had been corrected on the first unit, it was put through its final Syncrude acceptance test in December 1997, which it passed with flying colors.

In May 1998, O&K delivered its second RH400 to Syncrude's Base Mine operations, which was the first for Terex Mining. This unit, 11-36, was also equipped with the Cummins K2000E engines,

Terex O&K RH400E

The RH400E is equipped with a 56-cubic-yard bucket and is capable of handling an 80-ton payload. The giant front shovel generates a tremendous breakout force, which enables it to dig through the toughest of materials quickly. *ECO*

but they had a little more power dialed in, now with 3,650 flywheel horsepower available. By the end of 1998, the first RH400, 11-35, was finally retrofitted with the far more powerful QSK60 diesels, which raised its power output to 4,000 flywheel horsepower. A few months after this, 11-36 also had its engine package changed out for the more powerful QSK60 type.

Syncrude put in orders for two more RH400s for its new Aurora Mine operation. Both of these units, 11-37 and 11-38, had quite a few major upgrades made to them, including a longer boom, newly designed undercarriages, raised cabs, and 56.9-cubic-yard buckets. But the biggest change came with the engine package, which now consisted of two Caterpillar 3516B,

16-cylinder diesels, with increased power ratings of 4,400 flywheel horsepower (4,600 gross). All of these changes helped bring these new RH400s' operating weights up to 985 tons. Delivery of the 11-37 was in April 2000, with 11-38 following in May.

The fifth unit to be built, the RH400E, left the Dortmund factory in May 2000 destined for Kennecott Energy's Jacobs Ranch Mine in the Powder River Basin (PRB) mining area of Wyoming. Placed into service in July, it was the first of the series to be electric powered. It had two electric motors, producing 3,200 kilowatts equivalent to 4,291 horsepower. The RH400E was also equipped with a 56-cubic-yard bucket. Total operating weight of the electric version is

976 tons. It was also the first machine in the series to be painted in Terex Mining's corporate colors of white with red striping. In May 2001, the RH400E was moved from its first home to the Antelope Mine in the PRB, also a Kennecott Energy property, to help meet production demands at that facility.

In 2002, Terex Mining sold its sixth O&K RH400. As with the first four machines, this unit was to be delivered for work to the oil sand mining region of Northern Alberta. But this time the customer was the North American Construction Group, a major subcontractor to the large oil sand operations. This RH400, specially ordered for work at the new Muskeg River Mine, located near Mildred Lake, benefits from all of the experience gained from the earlier units. Engineers reworked many areas of the RH400's design, including the undercarriage

and engine bay. Once again, it was powered by two Cummins QSK60-C diesels, but this time with 4,400 flywheel horsepower available. Specified bucket capacity is listed at 56.9 cubic yards, with a maximum 94-ton payload limit. With all of the improvements made to this latest RH400, operating weight increased to a record-breaking 1,108 tons, the most for any hydraulic excavator. Not only was the RH400 the first hydraulic excavator to break the 900-ton barrier, it was also the first to smash the 1,000-ton barrier as well. This new giant was dedicated into service in January 2003.

No matter what the future holds in store for the RH400, its place in the earthmoving record books is ensured. But will a hydraulic excavator design like the RH400 ever catch up to an electric cable mining shovel in weight and capacity? Only time, and the marketplace, will tell.

Terex O&K RH400

In December 2002, Terex Mining delivered its sixth RH400 excavator to the North American Construction Group for work at the new Muskeg River Mine, located near Mildred Lake, Alberta. This RH400 is equipped with a pair of Cummins QSK60-C diesels, rated at 4,400 flywheel horsepower. Its overall working weight is 1,108 tons, the most of any of the RH400s. Bucket capacity is 56.9 cubic yards, with a maximum 94-ton payload limit. The shovel was officially dedicated into service in January 2003. Also that year, Terex Mining changed the nomenclature of the RH400 to TME400. *Gary Middlebrook*

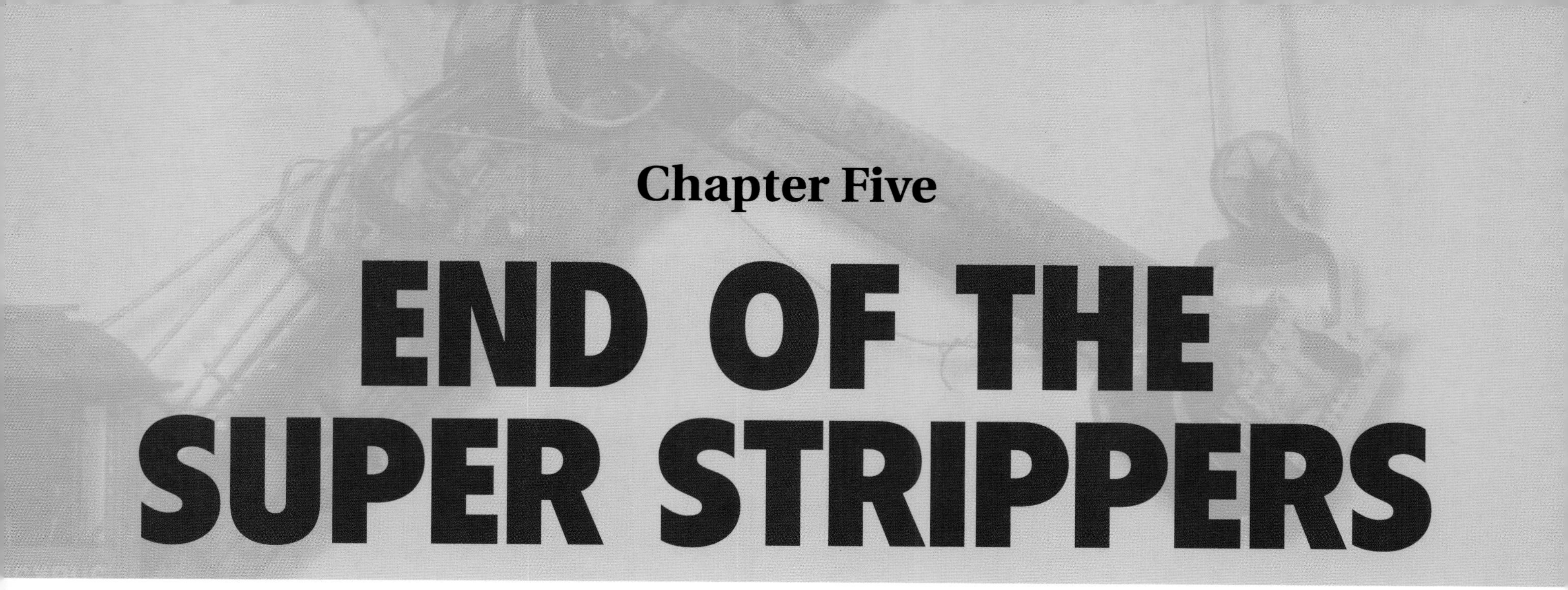

Chapter Five

END OF THE SUPER STRIPPERS

n 1971, the Marion Power Shovel Company delivered its last super-stripping shovel, a Model 5900, to the AMAX Leahy Mine in southern Illinois. Not only was it to be the last of its type produced by Marion, it was the last of its kind from any manufacturer. It seems the era of the super-stripping shovel ended as fast as it began. Though these magnificent shovels were the best of their breed, the mining industry ultimately chose the walking dragline as the preferred method of reaching deeply buried coal seams.

Even though the shovel and dragline had been allies over the decades, in many instances working side by side in mining operations across the United States, the greater working range of the dragline would ultimately prove too much for the shovel to overcome. As mining operations began to exhaust the easily recoverable coal deposits that were covered by a thin layer of overburden, the economics of coal mining dictated that a walking dragline of substantial size would be needed. Mining companies would have to dig deeper than ever before to reach new coal deposits. In many cases, land that had been previously mined by a stripping shovel would be revisited by a much larger walking dragline, to uncover even more coal deposits that were simply not economical to recover with a stripping shovel.

The reason for the dominance of the stripping shovel over the dragline for a good part of the 20th century was simply economics. Since the coal deposits were still relatively close to the surface, the digging characteristics of the stripping shovel met the needs of the industry. But as our appetite for energy increased in America, so did the need for fossil fuel, especially coal. The only thing that could possibly meet future digging requirements was the dragline. Though the super-stripping shovels held the edge for most of the 1960s, the writing was on the wall as to what the future would hold for these behemoths. This came into sharper focus in 1969, when Bucyrus Erie commissioned its 4250-W dragline at American Electric Power Company's (AEP) Muskingum Mine, near Zanesville, Ohio. Christened "Big Muskie," it carried a monstrous 220-cubic-yard bucket, which actually made the massive 180-cubic-yard dipper on the mighty Marion 6360 "Captain" shovel seem a bit on the small side, if such a thing was even possible. The crown of the largest earthmoving machine was now bestowed upon a walking dragline. Never again would the super-stripping shovel bask in the limelight as it once did in the mid-1960s.

With the walking dragline's unsurpassed working range, it was able to dig deeper than any shovel

Bucyrus Erie 1850-B "Brutus"
The only "super-stripping" shovel preserved for public display is the Bucyrus Erie 1850-B originally built for the Pittsburg and Midway Coal Mining Company in 1963. P&M donated the shovel in 1983 to the nonprofit organization of Big Brutus, Inc., which was entrusted with the care and restoration of the giant. In 1985 the shovel was opened to the public. It is shown here in August 1998. *ECO*

Marion 5761

Sahara Coal Company of Harrisburg, Illinois, first placed its Marion 5761 shovel to work in 1963. But by the late 1980s, its working days were through. It is shown here parked in the Sahara pit in November 1990. By the end of 1993, it would be gone. *Mike Haskins*

could ever dream of, and do it in such a way that its working area did not infringe upon the machine itself. Since the stripping shovel worked on top of the coal seam as it removed overburden, the dragline worked above it, on a specially prepared bench. This allowed the dragline to use its superior boom length to deposit overburden into spoil piles much farther away from the actual working area. With a stripping shovel, the spoil piles were right behind it. Because of the shovel's shorter working radius, the spoil could not be deposited any farther away, which often caused problems when parts of the spoil pile periodically slid back into the pit. When this happened, the shovel, along with any miners around it, could be put in harm's way. With the dragline, this problem was greatly reduced.

It seems that after 1969, mining owners that once only considered stripping shovels for their operations now were only more than happy to embrace a large walking dragline instead. Even as the last super-stripers were being built and delivered, draglines of equal or greater capacity were on the drawing boards at both Marion and Bucyrus Erie. In 1971, Marion introduced its popular 8750 series. Bucyrus Erie followed in 1972 with the release of a similar-sized model identified as the 2570-W. Both of these designs were capable of nominal bucket capacities of 115 cubic yards. Some models received smaller buckets, and others larger, but most were in the range of approximately 100 to 135 cubic yards. With draglines of this capacity now available, there simply was no need for any further stripping shovel production.

There is no argument from anyone that Big Muskie was the undisputed world's champ for a single-bucket digging machine. But could a manufacturer have built a super-stripping shovel that was even larger than the big 220-cubic-yard dragline? Well, Bucyrus Erie, the builder of Big Muskie, actually proposed a shovel in the early 1960s that was far more monstrous than even the 4250-W dragline. In mid-1963, while Marion was in the early design stages of the 180-cubic-yard 6360 shovel, Bucyrus Erie proposed a massive stripping shovel concept design of its own. Identified as the 4950-B, it was the company's answer to the Marion 6360, only larger. It was to have had a 250-cubic-yard dipper, capable of an unheard of capacity of 375 tons. Its operating radius would have measured 448 feet from the digging face to the spoil dump. The housing itself would have been supported by 16 crawlers, 4 per corner, with each truck measuring 41 feet, 5 inches in length. The working weight of the 4950-B was calculated at a whopping 18,000 tons. In comparison, Big Muskie weighed approximately 14,000 tons, while the 6360 Captain shovel tipped the

Bucyrus Erie 1650-B
United Electric Coal Companies operated two 70-cubic-yard Bucyrus Erie 1650-B shovels in Illinois. One was at its Buckheart Mine in Canton, and the other was located at its Fidelity Mine near Du Quoin. Pictured in November 1990 is the Fidelity shovel as it nears the end of its operating life. *Mike Haskins*

Bucyrus Erie 1650-B
By 1992, the 1650-B shovel at United Electric Coal Companies' Fidelity Mine had been taken off line and parked. In 1995 it was dismantled and scrapped. Its sister machine at the Buckheart Mine was parked in 1984 and was eventually sold off to Green Coal around 1993 to be used as spare parts for its two 1650-B shovels. Green Coal also bought most of the usable parts of the Fidelity Mine's 1650-B as well. But by the mid-1990s, both of Green's 1650-Bs were also shut down and scrapped. Today, none of the original five 1650-B shovels built by Bucyrus Erie survives. *Mike Haskins*

Marion 5761

Peabody Coal Company operated seven of the 15 Marion 5761 shovels built. The machine pictured here in October 1989 was originally put into service at Peabody's Warrior Mine in Alabama in 1967; it was equipped with a 75-cubic-yard dipper, one of the largest ever fitted on a 5761 series machine. In 1976 this 5761 was moved to Peabody's Alston Mine in Kentucky. This machine was officially shut down in 1986. Though offered for sale as late as 1992, it was scrapped by the mid-1990s. *Mike Haskins*

scales at about 15,000 tons. And the cost? The 4950-B was priced at an estimated 45 cents a pound, plus electrical equipment, which equaled $16.2 million in 1963 dollars—simply a huge sum at that time. In today's dollars, the cost of the 4950-B would have been well over $125 million. But it was not to be. It was simply too large and expensive for its time. Though Bucyrus Erie proposed the concept to a few mining operations that could handle (and afford) such a digging machine, none would sign on the dotted line. So ended the short design life of the 4950-B.

Even though deliveries of new stripping shovels ceased after 1971, this did not make the units already in the field obsolete all at once, since most of the shovels built would work out their days until the mines they worked at reached their economical ends. Once the available coal deposits had been exhausted from the mining operation, the shovel in all likelihood would have been parked to await disposition—usually the scrapper's cutting torch. For some shovels, the end came quickly. For others, a long wait in an empty field, or flooding pit, would be the norm. And still others would

Marion 5960 "Big Digger"

Peabody Coal's Marion 5960 "Big Digger" originally shipped from the factory in April 1969 and was up and running at Peabody's River Queen Mine in Kentucky by the end of that year. In 1988 the River Queen's mining operations were suspended. In 1989 the dismantling of the 9,338-ton 5960 was started. By the end of 1990 it was all gone. It is shown here with its boom lowered in October 1989. *Mike Haskins*

Marion 5761 "Stripmaster"
It was hoped that Peabody Energy would someday put the mighty Marion 5761 "Stripmaster" back into service after it was parked in 1991, but the lackluster coal market of the day sealed its doom and it was scrapped in 1998. It is shown here parked in May 1995. *ECO*

meet untimely ends because of accidents and fires. Only a few would escape the cutting torch as the 20th century came to a close.

Starting in the mid-1980s and continuing through the 1990s, one after another of the super-stripping shovels met their demise. The amended Clean Air Act of 1990 limited the use of high-sulfur coal in power plants. The coal was more commonly found in the Midwest of the United States. The mines found there were often older, well-established operations and were home to the majority of the super strippers. As more customers switched over to buying coal from the western part of the country, which mined a more environmentally friendly low-sulfur coal, many of the older surface operations began to wind down their activities. As these operations began to close their doors, most of the mining equipment was sold off to work another day—all, that is, except for the super-stripping shovels. Their size and age made them too costly to dismantle, transport, and reassemble at another location. Though many of the walking draglines from these mines eventually found new homes, the mighty shovels were left behind to be disposed of for their scrap-metal value. Shovels, whose very size and presence

Above: **Marion 5760 "Mountaineer"**
The Marion 5760 "Mountaineer" spent its last few years parked in a field just outside of Cadiz, Ohio, after being shut down in January 1979 due to the closing of the Egypt Valley Mine. It was scrapped in late 1988. Here, the Mountaineer is shown basking in the sun on a warm summer's day in July 1983. *Keith Haddock*

Bucyrus Erie 1950-B "GEM"
CONSOL parked the "GEM" in August 1988 after its working days were finished at the Mahoning Valley Mine No. 33 in Cadiz, Ohio. CONSOL had decided that only one of its Bucyrus Erie 1950-B stripping shovels was going to be needed for future operations. For the "Silver Spade" to live, the "GEM" had to be sacrificed. *Jon Kus*

when new staggered the imagination, were now nothing more than a nuisance that needed to be eliminated off the accountant's record books. The giant Bucyrus Erie 3850-B Lot I shovel, from Peabody's Sinclair Mine, met its end in 1986, as did CONSOL's mighty Marion 5760 Mountaineer in late 1988. Other super-stripping shovels that came to an end during this time were Peabody River Queen Mine's Marion 5960 Big Digger, scrapped in late 1989; CONSOL's Bucyrus Erie 1950-B GEM, scrapped mid-1991; Peabody's Bucyrus Erie 3850-B Lot II River King No. 6 shovel, scrapped 1993; Green Coal Panther Mine's Bucyrus Erie 1050-B, scrapped 1993; United Electric Fidelity Mine's Bucyrus Erie 1650-B, scrapped 1995; and the Marion 5761 Stripmaster from Peabody's Lynnville Mine, which was disposed of in 1998. Still more would come to know the heat of the scrapper's torch. CONSOL's Marion 5761 from its Burning Star No. 2 Mine, Sahara Coal's Marion 5761, Green Coal's two Bucyrus Erie 1650-B shovels, and Arch Coal's Marion 5900 and 5761, would all cease to exist in the 1990s. The list goes on, but the worst blow of all came on September 9, 1991, when a fire at the Captain Mine claimed the mightiest shovel of them all, the Marion 6360.

Bucyrus Erie 1950-B "GEM"
This close-up detail of the "GEM" in April 1990 highlights the lower works of the giant shovel including its front power cable reel. Many of the shovel's motors were saved as spare parts for the "Silver Spade," including two entire crawler truck assemblies. Starting in mid-1991, the demolition crews started to work on the giant. By early 1992, the task was complete. The GEM was no more. *Dale Davis*

Marion 6360 "The Captain"
On September 9, 1991, the Marion 6360, better known as "The Captain," was mortally wounded by a fire in its swing-circle area in its lower works. Deemed too expensive to salvage, it is shown here in July 1992, awaiting disposition. *ECO*

Marion 6360

As the months passed, workers mined around the stricken shovel, leaving it behind as operations at the Captain Mine continued on. Demolition of the shovel commenced in late 1992 and finished by early 1993. *ECO*

The Marion 6360, or Captain shovel, with its 180-cubic-yard dipper, was without question the biggest shovel ever to be put into service. Since 1965, its home was the Captain Mine. Except for the periodic shutdowns for maintenance, both minor and major, the shovel really never suffered any prolonged idleness. When it was down, its repairs were sometimes astronomical in price, but when it was working it was unmatched for its digging capabilities. It was a one-of-a-kind machine without peer in the world of shovels.

But all of that came to an end on that fateful September day, when workers on the afternoon shift noticed smoke coming out of the giant shovel's lower works. The news quickly spread over the radios to every point on the mine site that the 6360 was on fire. Emergency crews and equipment were dispatched immediately to the shovel's pit to battle the blaze. Smoke was billowing from various sections of the housing, with flames shooting out the lower left front of the shovel, just to one side of the operator's cab. The shovel was not totally engulfed in flames, as one might imagine. The majority of the flames were confined to the front of the behemoth. But the fire was hard to put down. On through the night, fire trucks, water tankers, and whatever else could be brought to bear were used in the fight to save the mighty Captain. By morning, the fire was out, but the damage had been done. As workers came in for the early shift, they were more quiet than usual. Many couldn't believe the 6360 was truly lost. It was as if someone very important had died that morning. Workers at the mine looked up to the 6360 with pride. It was the centerpiece of the entire mining operation and the principal stripping shovel as well. Not only did the workers feel they had lost a close friend, many others wondered if this would be the end of their livelihoods as well.

During the blaze, four members of the shovel's crew were trapped momentarily on the machine. Because of smoke and flames within the housing, they were not able to exit the shovel by way of its center elevator. But one by one, the crew was brought down by ropes and harnesses to safety. None was seriously injured in the ordeal. But the damage to the shovel itself was extensive. From the outside, the 6360 looked intact. But its interior, especially in the lower works, was another story. Because the fire was so deep within the shovel itself, it was hard to put water where it would do the most good.

In the weeks to follow, investigators and engineers from both Marion and Arch surveyed the damage. It was believed that a high-pressure hydraulic line had burst in the lower section of the shovel in the swing-circle area. It is theorized that the broken line released a fine mist of hydraulic fluid that was ignited by a spark produced by the opening and closing of circuit breakers also found in this area of the shovel. The 6360 had few compartments separating the hydraulic systems from the electrical. (Later stripping shovels built by

Top: Marion 6360
As if it were getting ready for the next big bite of overburden, the mighty 6360 held its massive 180-cubic-yard dipper aloft until the end. To the right of the operator's cab can be seen the scorched burn mark just above where the fire had exited the lower works of the shovel. *ECO*

Right: Marion 6360
The crawler assemblies on "The Captain" were the largest ever installed on a stripping shovel. Each section was 45 feet long, 10 feet wide, and 16 feet high. Each crawler carried 42 track pads, weighing 3.5 tons apiece. Crawler assemblies this large were needed to support the shovel's entire massive weight of 15,000 tons, the most for any mobile land machine even to this day. *ECO*

Demag H485

The original diesel-powered Demag H485 front shovel was shipped over from the United Kingdom in 1995 for work at Suncor Energy's oil sands mining operation, located just north of Fort McMurray, Alberta, Canada. It worked for the next two years as a stockpile shovel until finally being shut down in early 1997. It is shown here in October 1997 at Suncor's "boneyard," being dismantled for spare parts to be utilized on the company's other Demag H485, which is electric powered. Only a few bits and pieces remain today. *ECO*

Marion 291-M

After some 35 years of faithful service for Peabody and its western subsidiary, Powder River Coal, both of the Marion 291-M long-range coal-loading shovels were parked at the end of 1997. Today, they sit on an isolated part of the North Antelope Rochelle Complex in Wyoming, awaiting an uncertain future. They are pictured here in October 1998. *ECO*

Marion had these areas isolated to reduce the chance of an accident getting out of hand.) Once the fire had started, it found ready fuel in the large amounts of grease that had built up over the years in the swing-circle area. This kept the fire burning and made it extremely difficult to extinguish. Marion engineers concluded that the shovel could be repaired for around $2 million, but would not guarantee that the shovel would work as before, if at all. If the shovel should start up, move a few paces, and then fall over, it would be Arch that would be left holding the bag. In the end, Arch decided that it was just too big of a financial gamble to try to repair the 6360. With the life of the mine itself nearing an end in the next few years, Arch concluded that the best course of action was to dispose of the shovel where it sat, for its scrap metal value.

In July 1992, I made my last trip down to the Captain Mine to view the 6360 before the demolition teams moved in to have their way with her. To take up the production slack left vacant by the shovel, the mine's 105-cubic-yard Marion 5900 was rerouted to the 6360 pit. The 5900 would dig around the 6360 and leave it somewhat hidden within the mine itself. As we approached the 6360, it was partially encircled by the spoil piles made by the 5900 as it continued its business of uncovering coal seams to be removed. As I approached the once mighty shovel, I was in total amazement at the sheer size of it. Standing beside the shovel's crawler and looking straight up 21 stories, all one sees is shovel. This is truly the most awe-inspiring machine I have ever witnessed. I have often been asked which was the most impressive machine to see in person: Big Muskie or the Captain shovel? Both are huge machines, but the Marion 6360 has always struck me as the most imposing of the two. This is not to say Big Muskie wasn't similarly large; it was, but in different ways. Big Muskie looked more like a warehouse with a large boom attached to it. Its locomotion was more abstract because of the use of walking shoes. People seeing Big Muskie for the first time were mostly unaware how the behemoth got around, let alone how it worked. But on the 6360, there was no mistaking it for anything else but a shovel. With its eight massive crawler track assemblies, the shovel resembled something out of a science fiction novel. You could imagine this thing moving along the ground, as its dipper teeth cut into the highwall, extracting hundreds of tons of material per bite. It was the Mike Mulligan steam shovel story brought to its final realization. It was a machine that challenged the imagination. It was the ultimate shovel.

Bucyrus Erie 200-B
On permanent display at the Reynolds Alberta Museum, located in Wetaskiwin, Alberta, is this rare 372-ton, 1929-vintage Bucyrus Erie 200-B stripping shovel. It is shown at sunset in October 1997. *ECO*

Bucyrus Erie 200-B
The Bucyrus Erie 200-B was rated as a 5-cubic-yard shovel when it was originally introduced in 1927. In production until 1943, only 13 class 200-B shovels and 7 class 200-B draglines were ever built. This 1929 model stripping shovel is the last of them. *ECO*

Strewn around the grounds by the shovel were remnants of the fire, such as depleted fire extinguisher bottles. Underneath the shovel itself were massive pools of melted aluminum that had rained down from the shovel's upper sections during the height of the inferno. Traveling upward into the base of the shovel, one can clearly see 6-inch structural I-beams that had deformed and twisted from the intense heat. An auxiliary power line had been hooked up to the shovel to keep some of the lights, as well as the center personnel elevator, in operation. Once inside the claustrophobic elevator, one was immediately overwhelmed by the acidic smell of smoke which permeated the insides of the shovel. From the elevator, you stepped into the main machinery housing. Other than the smell of smoke, the fire left only minor damage, since the majority of the flames were below deck.

The interior had now become a sort of aviary, with chirping birds gliding around everywhere. Many of the 6360 shovel's steel siding panels on the right side had been removed to let light into the housing to allow personnel to survey the damage.

This allowed birds to take up residence within, as they made their nests along the upper rafters of the housing. The extra light afforded by the missing panels also aided in the removal of many of the shovel's electric motors. These would have monetary value on the open market. But the largest of these motors, such as the massive hoist units, could not find a home. These needed a customer with similar-sized equipment that could use such large and powerful electric motors. About the only possible customer for these was AEP for use in Big Muskie. But since that shovel had been idled in 1991, AEP was not in the market for any spare parts.

Sitting in the operator's cab, one got a bird's-eye view of the ultra-large 180-cubic-yard dipper as it hung in the air, frozen in time. Parts of the control panels were missing, as was the seat, but all of the windows were intact. From the cab, the view was quite impressive, with little to get in the way of the operator's line of sight. One could easily imagine oneself at the controls of this mighty beast, as it crowded the bucket into the highwall and hoisted it skyward. Being an operator of the 6360 was one of the top seniority assignments offered by the mine. Only the most skilled and experienced personnel were allowed to take full control of the shovel's estimated 15,000 tons of steel bulk. Many considered it a privilege to be entrusted with the operation of such a machine. Most would consider it the highlight of their careers. And none would be sorrier to see it go than these operators and their ground crews. For years they kept the 6360 in operation, around the clock, month after month, year after year. But now, it was out of their hands.

It was still hard to believe that the shovel would not work again. From the outside, it looked like it was about to go back to work. Just a few minor repairs, some paint, and it would be as good as new. But its internal injuries were mortal. There was nothing left to do but dispose of the body, so to speak, and this would get underway in late 1992. By mid-1993, the shovel was gone. Nothing was saved for posterity's sake: not a set of crawlers, not even the giant dipper. The mine did not want any spectators entering the property to view artifacts of the shovel left behind. After all, they were a coal mining company, not a museum. The only thing that was salvaged from the Captain shovel was the American flag that was flying on her at the time of the fire. It was preserved at the mine office reception area until operations at the Captain Mine were shut down permanently in the late 1990s. With the mine closed and reclamation of the mining property completed, all that is left is pastures of green grass. It is hard to imagine that there is no trace of something as large as the 6360 ever having been here, except in the form of still photographs and some rare video footage. There is no memorial, no monument, nothing to indicate that the world's largest shovel made its home near Percy, Illinois, for some 27 years. It's gone, and in the not-too-distant future, so will be most of the memories of one of the greatest earthmoving machines ever conceived and built by man.

As we enter the 21st century, only three of the large stripping shovels survive in operable condi-

Right: **Marion 360**
The 8-cubic-yard Marion Model 360 shovel, pictured here in October 1997, is the centerpiece of the Diplomat Mine Museum, located in Forestburg, Alberta. Perfectly restored to its former glory, it stands as a monument in recognition of the thousands of men and women who have worked in Canada's coal mining industry over the decades. *ECO*

Left: **Marion 360**
This 1927-vintage Marion Model 360 stripping shovel actually started life as a dragline and then was converted to a shovel. Normally, the stripping shovel version of this excavator was identified as the Model 350. Produced between 1923 and 1941, there were 35 Model 350 shovels and 12 Model 360 draglines placed into service. *ECO*

Bucyrus Erie 1850-B "Brutus"
Bucyrus Erie's 1850-B "Brutus" shovel is on display at the Big Brutus Museum located near West Mineral, Kansas, on the far eastern side of the state. The museum is open year round. Visitors can actually board the giant shovel and climb all the way to the top of the boom, which is some 16 stories in the air. It is preserved in its original P&M orange-and-black paint scheme. *ECO*

tion: Peabody Energy's Marion 5900, Freeman United's Bucyrus Erie 1050-B, and CONSOL's Bucyrus Erie 1950-B "Silver Spade." Of these three shovels, two are currently working, and one is parked. The Marion 5900 that worked at Peabody's Lynnville mining operations was idled in December 1999 after the company closed the mine due to the low cost of coal on the open market. Even though the operations are shut down, Peabody has kept the infrastructure intact, including all of the capital equipment required to go back to full operations in case of an improving coal market. The 112-cubic-yard (originally 105) 5900 shovel sits in a pit at the Lynnville operations, waiting for the day it goes back to work. Only time will tell if this is to be.

The other two stripping shovels have had better luck than Peabody's 5900, but both have had their close calls nonetheless. Freeman United's Bucyrus Erie 1050-B is the oldest operating of the two shovels. It originally began work in 1960 at United Electric Coal Companies' Banner Mine. In 1982 it started operations with a new owner, Freeman United at its Industry, Illinois, mine location. This particular Bucyrus Erie 1050-B was the last of its model type built by Bucyrus Erie and was the last of its rear-counterweight-designed machines. With a design that dates back to 1941, this shovel is about as low tech as they come, but it is this shovel's simplicity that has kept it producing over the years as its much larger counterparts have gone the way of the scrapper's torch. The shovel for the most part has worked around the clock since 1982. There have been periodic shutdowns over the years for maintenance, mine slowdowns, and the occasional labor dispute, but the shovel always went back to work. Things were starting to look grim for the shovel, as well as the mine itself, in the late 1990s, when there were talks of shutting the mine down after one of its coal contracts was not renewed. But in due time, new contracts were secured, which gave new life to the miners, as well as the shovel itself. At the time of this writing, the mine has a solid contract in hand and work for the last of the 1050-B shovels. It is hoped that the shovel will work to 2004 and beyond. In the end, it will be the marketplace that ultimately decides the fate of the 1050-B and the Industry Mine. But for now, it is work as usual.

The last of the working stripping shovels is CONSOL's Bucyrus Erie 1950-B, better known as the Silver Spade. This 105-cubic-yard shovel is presently the only super stripper in operation. If Peabody's 5900 never is put back to work, the Silver Spade will be known as the last as well. Since being dedicated in November 1965, it has been one of CONSOL's most dependable shovels. Over the years, the Silver Spade has been one of many CONSOL stripping shovels to work in the Cadiz, Ohio, area. Shovels such as the GEM of Egypt and the legendary Mountaineer worked in the same vicinity as the Silver Spade. Now only the Spade remains. The shovel has had some lengthy shutdowns over the years. The longest of these started in October 1982 and ended in April 1989. This shutdown had more to do with the economics of coal mining at the time, and not with the shovel itself. In 2001, the shovel was moved to a new mining location at CONSOL's Mahoning Valley mining operations near Cadiz. But by June 2002, the shovel had been parked because of a glut of unsold coal stockpiles. In October 2002, as another winter approached, coal demand had increased, and the Silver Spade was once again "swinging" in the pit. As long as there's a demand for the coal from Mahoning Valley, the Silver Spade will be needed to uncover it.

For those wishing to get a firsthand look at one of these titanic shovels, there are three that have been saved for posterity here in North America. Two are in Canada, and the other is in the United States. The Canadian shovels are both in Alberta. At

Marion 5900

Peabody's Marion 5900 is currently the largest-capacity stripping shovel in existence. Although it was originally equipped with a 105-cubic-yard dipper, its bucket subsequently was enlarged to 112 cubic yards in the 1990s. After Peabody suspended its Lynnville mining operations in December 1999, the 5900 shovel was left parked in the pit on standby, just in case the mine's existing coal reserves were once again needed in the marketplace. As of 2003, the 5900 awaits an uncertain future and has had to bear the indignity of having its windows shot at and its wiring ripped out by vandals. It is shown here in May 1995 in all of its past glory. *ECO*

the removal of most of the internal electric motors, the shovel is complete and looks as good as it did on the day it first went to work in 1963. Located near West Mineral, Kansas, the Big Brutus Museum is open all year round to the general public. One can even climb to the top of the boom to get a view of the surrounding countryside that was once an active surface coal mining operation. Now, with all of the old mining property reclaimed, all that one sees is rolling fields of grass. Except for the shovel and its accompanying displays, one would never suspect that a coal mine was ever part of the existing landscape.

The future of the ultra-large stripping shovels is almost certainly extinction. Once the last of the operating stripping shovels reaches the end of its economic operating life, only the ones saved as museum pieces will be around to remind us of what once was.

On the other hand, the story concerning the large two-crawler loading shovels is still being written, with no apparent end in sight for either the cable or hydraulic machines. Though it is doubtful that loading shovels will ever approach the size of a super stripper, many of the structural designs of these titans will influence the design of future loading shovels. One of these concepts is the Bucyrus International 795-B design proposal, first put forth at the MINExpo 2000 show in Las Vegas, Nevada. The 795-B concept uses the best in current technology, as well as tried and proven designs from the past. Bucyrus not only can draw from its vast engineering designs both past and present, it can also incorporate the vast knowledge of Marion loading and stripping shovel technology. Bucyrus' acquisition of the Marion Power Shovel Company in 1997 leaves the South Milwaukee company holding all of the design patents for all of the super strippers ever produced, as well as its loading shovels. The 795-B is a two-crawler design, incorporating a knee-action front-end geometry with a deck-mounted hydraulic crowd mechanism. This design is not unlike the knee-action crowd designs found on some of the last super-stripping shovels built by both Bucyrus and Marion. The shovel design is capable of a nominal dipper capacity of 135 tons. This would allow the 795-B to load 240-ton-capacity haulers in two passes, 400-ton in three, and future generation 500-ton designs in four. Approximate working

Bucyrus Erie 1050-B

One thing you can say for sure, Freeman United Coal's Bucyrus Erie 1050-B is a survivor. Many times over in this shovel's life it seemed its working days had come to an end, only to get a reprieve when a new mining contract was secured. It has been in operation since 1960, first with United Electric Coal, then starting in 1982 with the Freeman United Coal Mining Company. Shown at work in October 2000 at the Industry Mine, located in Industry, Illinois, the shovel is currently in operation as of 2003. *Urs Peyer*

the Reynolds Alberta Museum in Wetaskiwin, one can find a 1929-vintage Bucyrus 200-B stripping shovel in restored condition. And at the Diplomat Mine Museum in Forestburg, a beautiful 1927 Marion 360 stripping shovel is the centerpiece of its collection of historical mining equipment.

But only in the United States can one see an actual super stripper on display. Referred to as "Brutus," it is a Bucyrus Erie 1850-B shovel that was built for the Pittsburg and Midway Coal Mining Company (P&M). Originally dedicated into service in May 1963, it worked for the next 11 years until it was shut down in April 1974. For the next few years, the shovel sat and awaited an uncertain future at P&M's Mine 19 in Hallowell, Kansas. In 1983, P&M donated the shovel, along with 16 acres of land surrounding it and a grant of $100,000 to Big Brutus, Inc., a special nonprofit organization set up to see to the restoration and eventual display of the giant machine. On July 13, 1985, the Bucyrus Erie 1850-B "Brutus," the name it was christened with when new, was officially dedicated as a permanent museum and memorial to the coal mining regions of Kansas. Except for

Bucyrus Erie 1950-B "Silver Spade"
As of 2003, the "Silver Spade" was the largest stripping shovel in operation in the world. With its 105-cubic-yard dipper, it keeps on digging for CONSOL at its Mahoning Valley mining operations just outside of Cadiz, Ohio. Though the mighty Spade was temporarily sidelined in June 2002, it was put back to work by October of that same year. It is shown at work here in August 1999. *Keith Haddock*

weight of the shovel is quoted at 2,250 tons. This would outweigh P&H's 5700XPA shovel by some 150 tons, making the 795-B the world's largest two-crawler loading shovel—if they ever build it, that is.

Two factors at the present time have kept the Bucyrus 795-B proposal from becoming a reality. One is lack of a customer. The other is that the current truck fleets in the world mining market are still too small in payload capacity to necessitate a loading shovel of this size to be produced in any numbers. Currently, the largest hauler on the market in series production is Caterpillar's 797B. With a nominal payload capacity of 380 tons, it would match up fairly well with the 795-B. But with so few of these haulers in the marketplace at the present time, the economics of taking the 795-B from concept to iron is still considered not feasible by the mining industry. As trucks the size of the 797-B and larger start to gain a wider acceptance from the bigger mining companies around the world, a shovel with the design and performance capabilities of the 795-B will be needed.

Bucyrus 795-B Concept
Though only a computer-drawn Solid Works image at this point, the Bucyrus 795-B concept, originally unveiled at the MINExpo 2000 held in Las Vegas, Nevada, gives good indications what the company's future shovel designs might look like. The 795-B, as illustrated here, is a 135-ton-capacity, 2,250-ton shovel. If built, it would be the world's largest loading shovel on two crawlers. All that stands in the way of the 795-B from becoming a reality is a paying customer.
Bucyrus International

Though the giant super-stripping shovels, with their massive dippers and eight crawlers, will soon go the way of the dinosaur, the two-crawler loading shovels just keep gaining in size to keep pace with the ultra-large haulers being fielded today. Whether cable or hydraulic, there is nothing else on the horizon that can take the place of the crawler-type loading shovel for large-volume digging. As the haulers grow ever larger, even more massive shovels will be needed to load them. It is doubtful, though, that the loading shovel concept will ever reach the size of a stripping shovel, or a super stripper, for that matter. It doesn't need to. The larger range of the strippers is not needed when the truck you are loading is parked next to you, as with the loading shovel. Though it will be sad to see the last of the super strippers one day silenced, the legacy of ultra-large, high-volume shovels will continue on with designs that maybe are not as awesome in size, but are faster, smarter, and more technologically advanced, making them the most productive shovels ever to walk the face of the earth.

BIBLIOGRAPHY

Farrell, William E. ***Digging by "Stame."*** Edited and revised by Donald W. Frantz. Grand Rapids, Ohio: Reprinted by the Historical Construction Equipment Association.

Grimshaw, Peter N. ***The Amazing Story of Excavators, Volume I: Makers of Machines that Reshape the World.*** Wadhurst, East Sussex, England: KHL Group, 2002.

Haddock, Keith. ***Extreme Mining Machines.*** Osceola, Wisconsin: MBI Publishing Company, 2001.

Haddock, Keith. ***Giant Earthmovers.*** Osceola, Wisconsin: MBI Publishing Company, 1998.

Marion Construction Machinery, 1884–1975 Photo Archive. Edited by the Historical Construction Equipment Association. Hudson, Wisconsin: Iconografix, 2002.

Williamson, Harold F., and Kenneth H. Myers, II. ***Designed for Digging.*** Evanston, Illinois: Northwestern University Press, 1955.

INDEX

Albanian Sands Energy, Muskeg River Mine, 99, 139
AMAX Coal Company, Belle Ayr Mine, 78, 80, 94
Eagle Butte Mine, 60, 61, 78, 80
Leahy Mine, 57, 141
American Electric Power Company (AEP), 152
Muskingum Mine, 141
Anamax Mining Company, Twin Buttes Mine, 87
AOKI Marine Company, 119
Arch Mineral Corporation, 51, 57, 82, 147, 151
Fabius Mine, 47
Ruffner Mine, 74, 85
ASARCO, 125
Mission Mine, 86, 87
Atlantic Equipment Company, 24
Austin-Western, 65
Ayrshire Collieries Corporation, Wright Mine, 47
B-L-H (Baldwin-Lima-Hamilton Corporation), 65
Baldwin Locomotive Works, 65
Ball Engine Company, see Erie Steam Shovel Company
Barnhart, Henry M., 19, 20
Barnhart's Steam Shovel and Wrecking Car, 20
Barnhart's Steam Shovel-Style A, 13, 20
Barrick Goldstrike, 73, 109, 113
BAUMA trade exposition, 109, 126, 136
Belleview Sand and Gravel, 17, 19, 22
Benjamin Coal Company, 105
Big Brutus, Inc., 141, 156
Blackwater Mine, 111, 120
Bloomfield Collieries, 75, 85
Boliden Mineral, Aitik Copper Mine, 107
Apirsa Zinc Mine, 124
Boston and Providence Railroad, 11, 13
Bucyrus Company, 24, 29, 30, 34, 62
Bucyrus Company, The, 16, 19–23, 28, 62, 73

Bucyrus Erie, 25, 27, 32, 34–37, 39–41, 44, 45, 49, 53–55, 57, 61–63, 66, 72, 75, 76, 80, 87, 89, 90, 112, 115, 116, 141–144, 156
Bucyrus Erie models, 20-H, 115
50-B, 10, 11, 14, 15, 17, 19, 20, 22, 25
71-B, 66, 75
88-B, 66, 67, 75
88-B Series III, 67, 75
120-B, 64, 73, 75, 76
150-BD "Doubler", 103, 115
190-B, 65, 75
190-BD, 115
200-B, 151, 152
295-B, 60, 61, 75, 79
350-H, 116
395-B series, 77, 87, 89
500-H, 116
550-B, 34, 39, 40
550-HS, 104, 116
750-B, 31, 34, 35
750-B Series II, 35–37
950-B, 32, 36, 37, 40
1050-B, 30, 32, 40, 41, 147, 154–156
1650-B, 37, 38, 44–46, 143, 147
1650-B dipper, 38
1650-B "Mr. Dillon", 39
1850-B "Brutus", 46, 49, 50, 140, 141, 154, 156
1950-B "GEM of Egypt", 51, 53, 55, 146, 147, 155
1950-B "Silver Spade", 49–55, 146, 154, 155, 157
2570-W, 142
3850-B Lot I "Big Hog", 42, 43, 47–49, 147
3850-B Lot II, 26, 27, 44, 45, 48–50, 56, 147
4250-B, 142–144
4250-W "Big Muskie", 141–143, 152
Bucyrus Foundry and Manufacturing, see The Bucyrus Company
Bucyrus International, 81, 84, 90, 91, 96
Bucyrus International 795-B design proposal, 156–158
Bucyrus International models,

495-BI, 81, 89
495-BII, 97–99
495HF, 98, 99
495HR, 96, 99
Bucyrus models, 78C, 16
80-B, 21, 22
100-B, 22, 24, 75
110-B, 75
150-B, 30, 75
175-B, 30
225-B, 30, 33
320-B, 29, 34
351M-ST, see 595-B
595-B, 84, 90, 91, 98, 99
No. 0, 15, 21
Bucyrus-Monighan, 62
Bucyrus-Vulcan Class 5, 28
Bucyrus-Vulcan Company, 24, 28, 62
Budge Mining, 126
Cabot Corporation, 120
Carmichael and Fairbanks, 11
Carnes, Harper and Company, see Lima Locomotive Works
Carney-Cherokee Coal Company, 30
Carter Mining Company, 91
Caterpillar, 128
Caterpillar models, 793B hauler, 60, 61
797 hauler, 95
5000 series, 128
5130, 128
5230, 116, 129
5230B, 130
Chapman, Oliver S., 13
Chile Exploration Company, 34
Clark 2400B-LS, 67
Clark Equipment, 65
Clark-Lima, see Clark Equipment
Clean Air Act of 1990, 146
Coal and Allied Industries, 76, 86
Coal Contractors, Ltd., 106
Colowyo Coal Company L.P., 81
CONSOL (Pittsburgh Consolidation Coal Company), 33, 36, 42, 43, 49, 53,

54, 55, 147, 155
Burning Star No. 3 Mine, 48, 53, 147
Butler Mine, 103
Egypt Valley Mine, 53, 55, 146
Georgetown No. 12 Mine, 36, 43
Mahoning Valley Mine No. 36, 52, 146, 155, 157
Red Ember Mine, 48, 53
Cyprus-Pima Mining Company, 79
Starfire Mine, 79, 80
Deadhead, 44
Demag (Mannesmann Demag Baumaschinen), 101, 105, 133, 134
Demag models, B504, 101, 103
H241, 105, 109, 119, 122
H285S, see Kamotsu PC4000
H455S, 124
H485 series, 106–108, 122, 125, 134, 150
H685S, 126, 127
H685SP, 134
Diplomat Mine Museum, 153, 156
Duensing, Paul, 36
Dunbar and Ruston Steam Navvy, 16
Dreadnaught shovel series, 25
E. H. France Company, 13
Eastwick and Harrison, 12, 13
Eells, Dan P., 16
Energy Fuels Mine, 70
Erie-A, 24
Erie-B, 24
Erie Steam Shovel Company, 24, 25, 62
Euclid FD, 63
Euclid R-45, 64, 66
Euclid R-62, 65
Fairview Collieries Corporation, Flamingo Mine, 41
Ferwerda, Ray, 101
Fording River Coal, 82, 89
Freeman United Coal Mining Company, 154
Industry Mine, 32, 41, 154–156
French, Charles Howe, 11, 12
General Machinery Corporation, see Lima-Hamilton Corporation